FACTFINDER GUIDE

DOGS

The publisher gratefully acknowledges the contribution of Animal Photography, who provided all the illustrations for this book:

Sally-Anne Thompson for pages front cover (top left, top right, bottom left), 2 (left), 3 (right), 6-7 (main), 7 (inset below middle), 7 (inset bottom), 10, 13, 18, 19, 22, 28-29 (main), 29 (all), 30, 31, 32, 33, 34, 35, 36, 37, 38, 39, 40, 42, 44, 45, 50, 51, 52, 53, 54, 55, 56, 57 (both), 57, 58, 59, 60, 62, 64, 65, 66, 67, 68, 69 (both), 71, 73, 74, 75, 76, 77, 78, 80, 82, 83, 84, 85, 86, 88, 89, 90, 91, 92, 93, 94, 96, 97, 98, 99, 101, 102, 103, 104, 106, 107, 108, 109, 110, 111, 113, 114, 115, 117, 119, 120, 121, 122, 123, 124, 125, 126, 127, 128, 129(bottom), 130, 131, 132, 133, 134, 138, 140, 141, 145, 148, 149, 151, 153, 154, 156, 157, 159, 160, back cover

R T Willbie for pages 2 (right), 3 (left), 7 (inset above middle), 7 (inset top), 14, 17, 23, 24, 27, 41, 43, 46, 47, 48, 49, 61, 63, 70, 72, 79, 81, 87, 95, 100, 105, 112, 116, 118, 129 (top), 137, 139, 142, 143, 144, 146, 150, 152, 155,

Paddy Cutts/Animals Unlimited for pages 135, 136, 158

Additional photography was provided by Ann Ghublikian front cover (bottom right)

FACTFINDER GUIDE

DOGS

Iain Thomson

THUNDER BAY
P·R·E·S·S

This edition published in 1999 by
Thunder Bay Press
5880 Oberlin Drive, Suite 400
San Diego, California 92121
1-800-284-3580

http://www.advmkt.com

Produced by
PRC Publishing Ltd,
Kiln House, 210 New Kings Road,
London SW6 4NZ

ISBN 1 57145 199 4
(or Library of Congress CIP data available on request)

1 2 3 4 5 99 00 01 02 03

Printed and bound in China

CONTENTS

INTRODUCTION

The dog, "a man's best friend," is an extraordinary animal; but what exactly is a dog? Specifically it is a carnivorous mammal (*Canis familiaris*) of the family *Canidae*, and the only member of the 38 species of *Canidae* that can be said to be fully domesticated. It is distinguished from other canines, like wolves and foxes, by its close association with humans and by the enormous genetic variability within the species. For over two centuries, arguments have raged as to whether the domestic dog originated from the wolf, *Canis lupus*, or the golden jackal, *Canis aureus*. Dogs can produce fertile hybrids with both the wolf and the jackal, suggesting to some experts that all three should be considered as a single species. The argument on the other side considers the dog, distinguished by its uniquely upturned tail, to be a separate species. It cannot be ruled out that dogs have descended from several species, extinct and recent, commingling together. In 1868 Darwin concluded "We shall probably never be able to ascertain their origin with certainty," but the most widespread and accepted view today places the wolf (*Canis lupus*) as the wild progenitor of the domestic dog.

Considering how long dogs have been an integral part of human society, it is surprising how few scientific studies have been carried out on the animal; historians and animal behaviorists have barely scratched the surface of the way our relationship with dogs has developed in the last 12,000 years. The behavioral patterns of wild animals such as wolves, foxes, and jackals have been studied and documented in great detail but it is startling how little we know about *Canis familiaris*. The only time the scientists seem interested in the species is when they substitute them for humans in biological or medical research. The relationship between man and dog is unique but its importance only really began to be realized after the Industrial Revolution had threatened its very existence. However, while Darwin studied domestic species like the dog when formulating his theories on evolution, modern scientists still seem to dismiss domesticated animals as somehow "unnatural" and therefore unsuitable for serious scientific study.

From as early as the Middle Pleistocene period, bones of wolves have been found in close proximity to the bones of early hominids. It is hypothesized that some wolf pups may have been kept by these early human family groups and been domesticated to a certain extent. Although these tamed wolves were many generations away from the true domesticated dog, they were its precursor.

Dogs have then, been part of human society for longer than any other domestic species and research concludes that they were first domesticated towards the end of the last Ice Age, when all human subsistence still depended on hunting and gathering. As humans became more sophisticated hunters, they developed more effective weapons to kill their prey. The success of long distance projectiles fired from a simple bow would have been enhanced by a new partnership with dogs that could help to track and bring down wounded animals. Both wolves and humans were accustomed to living in social groups and this cooperative hunting technique between human and dog resulted in far greater hunting efficiency. Given the success of this partnership, it is not surprising to find widespread respect and affection for hunting dogs throughout the world, especially in cultures where hunting is the primary form of subsistence.

Domestication of the dog was the result of biological and cultural processes working together. Biologically, in a sort of natural evolution, the species multiplied in numbers and was genetically changed by natural selection in response to prevailing conditions in the new, human, environment. The parent animals, having been isolated from the wild population formed a small founder group. At first this group would have been very inbred but, as the population grew, so natural selection took over. The cultural process began when the wolf was brought into the social structure of the human community. As the wolf became tamer, so it became less and less like its wild forbears as its variable characteristics changed in response to its new environment. The wolf was no longer a wild carnivore but, as part of human society, it became a dog. The immediate result of taming a wolf and inherently changing its diet was, within a few generations, a reduction in its size. There was a strong natural selection for diminution since smaller animals would have survived better on little food.

For centuries, in the later stages of domestication, humans have selectively bred dogs for special purposes — to pursue and retrieve game, as draft animals, and as guides. In time this selective breeding led to the development of the 400 or so different breeds of dog that inhabit the world today. A breed is a "relatively homogeneous group of animals within a species, developed and maintained by man." Humans, using selective breeding to get desired qualities, created each breed and the result is an almost unbelievable diversity of purebred dogs which will, when bred to others of their breed, produce their own kind. Working dogs are still used by such organizations as the military and the police while others are utilized by the blind as guide dogs or by farmers as herding dogs. Strict classification is difficult here as the German Shepherd (Alsation), for instance, was originally a herding dog but is now the most popular breed used by the police and the military as a guard dog. Many of these breeds no longer fulfil their original purpose and are now kept in city homes as much valued companions.

The widely held image of the dog as man's humble servant has not always been a strictly valid one. The dog has at various times in history been elevated to the position of a god or, indeed, been regarded as little more than a tasty ingredient for a stew. Generally, though, the dog has been much loved and admired for his hunting skills, companionship, as a source of warmth, and as an early warning system. As well as his strength, speed, and intelligence, his beauty has never lacked appreciation. The ancients — the Chinese, the Sumarians, the Egyptians, the Greeks, and the Romans — were all capable of admiring the beauty of dogs. Owning a good dog was a source of pride and owners would gather together to compare and discuss their favorites. By comparing their dogs, deciding which ones were best, and breeding from them, they could improve those qualities they found the most desirable.

So from the ancient cultures of the world until the present day people have taken great pride in the appearance of their dogs and have strived to improve them. Today, there are a great many organizations throughout the world dedicated to purebred dogs and their ownership. The oldest organization of its kind is The Kennel Club, founded in London in 1873, to legislate in canine matters. Among its earliest tasks was the compilation of a Stud Book which has been

GORDEN SETTERS at trials (see page 133)

published annually since then. In 1880, the Kennel Club introduced a system of "universal registration," and the ownership of purebred dogs has grown until today the number of dogs registered annually with the club exceeds 180,000. In all there are over two million dogs registered with the Kennel Club and it now recognizes 164 major breeds. The "standards" — specifications which detail a breed's essential features — are accepted by many worldwide kennel authorities as definitive statements on breeds. The standard is the "model" breeders use in their efforts to breed better dogs, and judges use it as a guide when evaluating dogs at a show. Each animal in competition is compared with the judge's mental image of the perfect dog described in the standard.

There are systems for classifying and breeding dogs throughout the world, many using a variation of the British system. The Kennel Club recognizes 164 major breeds classed in six distinct groups: Hound, Gundog, Terrier, Working, Toy, and so-called Utility or Non-Sporting. The Fédération Cynologique Internationale (FCI), which is the body covering most of the world outside the UK and North America, sub-divides the Working group into Working, Herding, and a separate sub-group to include Mastiff types. The American Kennel Club (AKC) was established in 1884, and is "Dedicated to Purebred Dogs and Responsible Dog Ownership." In the US, the AKC recognizes 146 of the known breeds and these are grouped into seven classes: Sporting, Hound, Working, Herding, Terrier, Toy, and Non-Sporting. There is also a Miscellaneous Class.

Sporting: Sporting dogs are naturally active and alert and make likeable, well-rounded companions. Members of the group include pointers, retrievers, setters, and spaniels. Remarkable for their instincts in water and woods, many of these breeds actively continue to participate in hunting and other field activities.

Potential owners of Sporting dogs need to realize that most require regular, invigorating exercise.

Hound: Most hounds share the common ancestral trait of being used for hunting. Some use acute scenting powers to follow a trail while others demonstrate amazing stamina as they pursue their quarry. This group encompasses quite a diverse lot including Pharaoh Hounds, Norwegian Elkhounds, Afghans, and Beagles, among others.

Working: Working dogs were bred to perform such jobs as guarding property, pulling sleds, and working with livestock. They have been invaluable assets to man throughout the ages and the group includes the Doberman Pinscher, Siberian Husky, and Great Dane, to name just a few. Quick to learn, these intelligent, capable animals make solid companions but their considerable dimensions and strength make many working dogs unsuitable as pets for average families. By virtue of their size alone, these dogs must be properly trained.

Herding: Created in 1983, the Herding Group is the newest AKC classification — its members were formerly of the Working Group. All breeds share the ability to control the movement of other animals. For example, the low-set Corgi, perhaps one foot tall at the shoulders, can drive a herd of cows many times its size to pasture by leaping and nipping at their heels. The vast majority of Herding dogs, as household pets, never cross paths with a farm animal but nevertheless, pure instinct prompts many of these dogs to gently herd their owners — especially the children of the family. In general, these intelligent dogs make excellent companions.

Terrier: Terriers are spirited, energetic dogs whose sizes range from fairly small, as in the Norfolk, Cairn, or West Highland White Terrier, to the magnificent Airedale Terrier. Their ancestors were bred to hunt and kill vermin, and terriers typically have little tolerance for other animals, including other dogs — many continue to project the attitude that they're always eager for a feisty argument. As a rule they make engaging pets, but require owners with the determination to match their dog's lively character.

Toy: The diminutive size of Toy dogs ensures they will always be popular with city dwellers and people without much living space. They make ideal apartment dogs, are very companionable, and training aside, it's easier to control a ten pound dog than one ten times that size.

Non-Sporting: Non-Sporting dogs are a diverse group including sturdy animals with as different personalities and appearances as the Chow Chow, Dalmatian, and French Bulldog. Some of these dogs, like the Schipperke and Tibetan Spaniel, are rare sights in the average neighborhood, while others, like the Poodle and Lhasa Apso, are quite popular. The breeds in the Non-Sporting Group are a varied collection in terms of size, coat, personality, and appearance.

Miscellaneous: A breed is admitted to this group when, in the judgement of the Board of Directors Authorities of the AKC, there is an active parent club with serious and expanding breeding activity over a wide geographic area. When the Board of Directors is satisfied that a breed is continuing a healthy, dynamic growth in the Miscellaneous Class, it may be admitted to registration in the Stud Book and the opportunity to compete in regular classes. Each group is based on the uses for which the breeds were originally developed and admission of a new breed to AKC's Stud Book is determined by the Board of Directors. Today, new breeds admitted for registry must have been well established in other countries for a significant period of time by registry organizations in those countries.

In 1929, the American Kennel Club (AKC) published its first edition of *The Complete Dog Book* which has been the premier reference on purebred dogs in America. Their latest edition, *The Complete Dog Book, 19th Edition, Revised* includes the seven breeds that gained AKC recognition since the 18th edition: the American Eskimo Dog, Australian Shepherd, Border Collie, Canaan Dog, Cavalier King Charles Spaniel, Greater Swiss Mountain Dog, and Shiba Inu. A Top Ten list of the most popular breeds in America, issued by the American Kennel Club in January 1998, shows that a wide variety of dogs are kept as pets in the United States.

1. Labrador Retrievers (for the seventh consecutive year in a row)
2. Rottweillers
3. German Shepherds
4. Golden Retrievers
5. Poodles
6. Beagles
7. Dachshunds
8. Cocker Spaniels
9. Yorkshire Terriers
10. Pomeranians

Is there such a thing as a perfect dog to own? The obvious answer is no! Many factors have to be taken into consideration; not least your living conditions and environment. Without stating the obvious, big dogs need more exercise and more space than little dogs.

Owning a dog can bring years of happiness as the special bond between humans and canine ensures great mutual benefit. However, to ensure the best relationship with your dog, you must be prepared for some important responsibilities. Have I found the right breed to fit into my lifestyle and home? Have I enough time to spend training, grooming, and exercising a dog? Am I willing to spend the resources to ensure the best future for a dog? Dogs in their natural state are pack animals and one of the worst forms of cruelty to animals is to keep a dog alone in a kennel. A dog needs constant social contact and it can never attain contentment if it is cut off from human and other animal interaction. It is generally agreed amongst animal behaviorists that if a puppy is given as much opportunity for bodily contact with human beings as possible during the decisive stages of its development, the closer the human-dog relationship will be.

The International Encyclopedia of Dogs (edited by Anne Rogers Clark & Andrew H. Brace) asks 20 questions of prospective dog owners, which they suggest the whole family should spend some time answering:

1. Has any family member owned a dog before?
2. Will someone be at home at all times?
3. Will the dog live in the house?
4. Will a fenced-in yard be provided?
5. Does any family member suffer from allergies to pets?
6. The initial cost of a dog is modest compared to its maintenance and care. Is the family able to meet the financial commitment?
7. Is the dog's size a consideration?
8. Is a vocal or quiet dog preferred?
9. Is any family member prepared to groom the dog's coat frequently?
10. What are the five essential traits this pet should possess?
11. Must this be a puppy and, if so, why?
12. If an adult dog is preferred, what are the age parameters: one year, two years etc?
13. Is the family familiar with an adult dog of the chosen breed?
14. Has a fancier been consulted about the breed's basic characteristics?
15. Has a veterinarian been consulted about the care and cost of a healthy dog?
16. Is there a preference for a male or female dog and, if so, why?
17. Is breeding the reason for owning a dog and, if so, will a responsible approach be taken toward this issue?
18. Is the pet to be neutered or spayed?

GLEN OF IMAAL TERRIER AND LITTER. This Breed, with its distinctive short legs, originated in Ireland where it was bred for hunting vermin and dog fighting competitions.

19. Will the animal be trained to be a good canine citizen?
20. Is there a true family commitment to taking care of the pet throughout all its years?

Having taken in these considerations, choosing the right breed of dog can be confusing. Great care and some research should be undertaken to ensure the right selection of dog for you and your family. The bonus of selecting a purebred dog is their predictability in size, coat, care requirements, and temperament. Knowing what your puppy will look like and the kind of care he or she will need as an adult is a key in selecting the breed for you. All too frequently, basic common sense goes by the board when selecting that cute little puppy. Buying a dog should be treated like any other purchase, the more knowledge you have of the product the more likely you are to make a sensible decision. Purchasing a dog is not the time to hunt for a bargain, as a new puppy should be a member of the family for its lifetime — upward of seven years — so you'll want to make a sensible investment. The purchase price of a puppy is not the only cost to be considered. It will need feeding and proper health care, and veterinary bills can be expensive. Take a good look at your financial affairs and make sure you can really afford a dog. A dog can bring great joy but it is also a huge responsibility. This applies to all aspects of acquiring a dog because it cannot, or definitely should not, be discarded if it does not come up to expectations. A dog is for life!

It cannot be overstressed that, when acquiring a pedigree dog, it is essential to buy a puppy from a responsible and well-respected breeder. A purebred dog is one that conforms to the standards of a certain breed and whose pedigree has been recorded for a certain period of time. It is essential with these dogs to insist that only those with proven qualities are used in breeding, otherwise the

ENGLISH FOXHOUNDS at a show (see page 75)

general quality of the breed may deteriorate. Responsible breeders are concerned with the improvement of the breed with an emphasis on breeding healthier dogs that have the appropriate temperament for their breed. Breeds of dogs are for the most part a modern invention, each breed created by humans using selective breeding to get desired qualities. The result is an almost unbelievable diversity of purebred dogs, which will, when bred to others of their breed, produce their own kind.

Through the ages, humans have designed dogs that could hunt, guard, or herd according to their needs. A good example of the way dogs have been bred for a specific purposes can be found in the sheepdog. Behaviorally there are two types of sheepdog, each type represented by a number of breeds. Both types of sheepdog have been selected to work with livestock but in two different ways. The duty of livestock guarding dogs is not to disrupt the sheep but to live among them and disrupt their predators. The duty of herding dogs on the other hand is to disrupt the behavior of the livestock and gather and lead them, on command, to another place. Although dogs are genetically programed to behave like dogs, different breeds display this program in different ways. Dog handlers can train working dogs based upon inherited, breed-specific behavior.

When the Kennel Club was founded in London in 1873, one of its early tasks, along with the compilation of the Stud Book, was to formulate an elementary code of rules relating to dog shows. The new club had records dating from 1859, when the first dog show was held at Newcastle-upon-Tyne with 60 entries of pointers and setters. Today, many varieties may be exhibited in the shows. A variety is a division of a breed for show purposes, based on coat type, size, or color. Dachshunds, for instance may be Longhaired, Smooth, or Wirehaired, and Collies may be Rough or Smooth. Members of different varieties of the same breed may be interbred and the offspring registered with organizations such as the Kennel Club and the AKC.

Showing a dog is not an easy task and there are many rigorous procedures to adhere to. In the first place an entry form with all the relevant data must be completed and the animal must have veterinary certificates certifying a clean bill of health. To be in show condition the dog must be absolutely free of parasites, it must not be in molt and its coat must be in perfect condition. The dog must also be obedient and highly trained — undisciplined behavior during the show will affect the judgement and may even lead to disqualification. Obviously, shows differ in grade and importance from small local shows to the highly important and prestigious national shows. Although there are no prizes or ribbons awarded, the most important shows are the club reviews. It is here that the qualities of young dogs are ascertained and breed assessors estimate their merits in terms of breeding.

Arguably, the most famous dog show in the world is "Crufts," which the Kennel Club has run since 1948. The show was founded by Charles Cruft, "The British Barnum," who had a remarkable flair for attracting publicity for his shows. Whilst working with the Canadian-born James Spratt in his dog biscuit company, Cruft started organizing terrier shows and, in 1891, ran his first show open to all breeds. Charles Cruft continued to run these shows personally until his death in 1938. Today, the Crufts Dog Show attracts visitors from all over the world and it annually draws in over 100,000 spectators. The Kennel Club now licenses over 7,000 events each year compared to fewer than 50 shows when the first Crufts took place in 1891.

There had been dog shows from the later years of the 18th century and throughout the first half of the 19th, but these early shows were interested only in what were termed Sporting Dogs. There were foxhound shows, gundog shows, and the darker world of dog fighting and baiting. It is worth noting that these early shows, attended by masters of foxhound packs, played an important role in the evolution of agriculture, helping to popularize the agricultural methods being developed in the latter half of the 18th century. At this time of great change people were also moving from the countryside to live in towns due to the Industrial Revolution, but were reluctant to give up their animals (it has been estimated that perhaps as many as every second household contained a dog). It was from the middle to the end of the 19th century that the interest in pet dogs began to develop and was epitomized by the formal dog shows and Crufts. The small urban shows for pet dogs continued to be held, as they are today, but the growing number of shows catering for all breeds attracting entrants from afar continued apace. Pedigree shows worldwide today encourage honest, fair competition based on sound and knowledgeable judgement and concentrate on improving the quality of purebred dogs.

In addition to the purebred dogs that are admitted into the various kennel clubs, there are many breeds that have a long history and are instantly recognizable, but which are not regarded as purebreds. One such example is the Jack Russell. The Parson Jack Russell Terrier, as it is formally known, was named after a theology student at Oxford who bred this distinctive strain of Fox Terrier over a period of more than 60 years. Both the Jack Russell and the modern Fox Terriers are all descended from the fox terriers of the late 18th and early 19th centuries. It is almost impossible to find documented pedigrees of before 1860, but we do know, from his biographer E.W.L. Davies, that John Russell acquired "Trump," his ideal terrier, in the spring of 1819. By the time of the Parson's death in 1883 there was an abundance of cross-bred hunt terriers, indiscriminate in size, referred to as Jack Russells. They are not purebred in the sense that they have a broad genetic make-up, a broad standard, and do not breed true to type.

A purebred dog is one with a proven pedigree, ideally from a good brood bitch and stud dog. The quality a bitch passes on is less a matter of her outward appearance — the phenotype — but more her ancestry — the genotype. The law of heredity establishes that the genetic qualities of an animal — the genotype — are largely dependent on the animal's ancestry. For centuries it was believed that the sire played the sole, decisive role in the breeding of animals, but it is now recognized that both the male and the female are equally responsible for the quality of their young. There is however, one very forceful and indisputable fact that supports the argument that the influence of stud dogs in breeding is considerably greater than bitches — one single dog might sire up to 1,000 puppies in a single year whereas the bitch could hardly bear 20.

The real question is whether the appearance and beauty of dogs is given more weight than qualities such as health, intelligence, and working ability. In most dog shows the sole criterion of the quality of the dogs is their beauty. This is fine if dogs are bred exclusively for the ring, but the problem is that most dogs are bred as family pets. In the interests of pet dogs, and those who buy pedigree puppies, people should not be misled into overrating those ideals of beauty set out in a breed standard, which, after all, is man-made.

At the present time dogs can be found in every part of the world where humans are also living. The domesticated dog is one of the most popular companion animals with an estimated population of 90 million in western Europe and the USA. One in every four households in western Europe owns a dog, and the figure rises to two in every five households in the USA. The relationship that began with tamed wolves has evolved over some 12,000 years to the stage where today the dog has become very important as an object of affection. Anthropomorphism is common to dog lovers, as is obvious in the human names they give their pets, "Bertie" or "Sally" for instance, and in the way the breeds are described. The American Kennel Club describes the ideal Rottweiler as "calm, confident, and courageous. . . with a self-assured aloofness that does not lend itself to immediate and indiscriminate friendships." The Kennel Club (England) describes the temperament of the Labrador Retriever as "Intelligent, keen, and biddable, with a strong will to please. . . kindly nature with no trace of aggression or undue shyness." These given characteristics can have no scientific basis, but the overwhelming tendency to "personify" dogs is unsurprising and perhaps an inevitable consequence of the relationships dog lovers have had with their animals down the centuries.

JACK RUSSELL TERRIER

Care and Training of Dogs

The diversity of dog breeds has no parallel in the animal world and, in choosing which type of dog to own, great consideration must be given to the care and attention it will need. Some dogs need a great deal of exercise, some don't; some dogs require a lot of space, others don't; some dogs have coats that need very little attention while others may need hours of grooming a week.

When purchasing a puppy, it is advisable to buy from a reputable breeder, as this will guarantee the pedigree of the parents and the health of the dog — few legitimate breeders will object to the puppy getting a clean bill of health from a veterinarian's check before purchase. The first three weeks of a puppy's life are critical, as this is the time that determines its survival chances. It is vital that the pups start to nurse as soon as possible to acquire the mother's protective immunities and if the litter is very large the puppies should be rotated as they suckle so they each get a fair deal. Newborns should be handled daily from birth to encourage the dog-human bond from the start. From the third to seventh week the puppy can smell, hear, and see and it begins to take a real interest in its environment. Kennel clubs recommend that the puppy is kept with its mother for about ten weeks after birth, if they stay in the litter longer than this they are likely to become more dog orientated than people orientated.

LABRADOR RETRIEVER as a guide dog (see page 120)

By this time, the pup should have had at least its first two immunization shots and will have some idea of being clean in its quarters. It is a big change for the little animals when they leave their mother and kennel; the new owner has to be very understanding and immediately assume a maternal role — it is during this vital period that the long term relationship between owner and dog will be forged. If acquiring an older dog, great care should be taken in establishing its early history. A totally kennel-raised puppy will rarely make a good house dog but a well brought up, house-trained dog is certainly worth considering. Neither puppies or older dogs should be introduced into the household at times of great stress or excitement — Christmas for example — but at times of quiet so they can adapt to their new surroundings in a calm atmosphere.

The amount of space a dog needs varies enormously according to the breed. Toy breeds do not require much more than a corner of their owner's living area, whereas large breeds such as St Bernards, Great Danes, and many of the larger Sighthounds require a great deal of freedom and would feel shut in and claustrophobic when limited to a city apartment or house. If the dog is to be kept outside the house, the breed and its purpose must be taken into account when the yard and kennel is built.

A kennel should not be a prison for the dog but a much-loved free area and a comfortable living space. A kennel in which the dog is to be left all year round must be thoroughly protected against the elements and should be shielded from the wind and shaded from the sun in the heat of the day. If the kennel is to be a temporary shelter, it can be quite a simple affair but if it is to house the dog permanently it should be large and solidly built. All dogs dislike damp and permanently shaded places but it is essential for hardy breeds such as sledge dogs or Newfoundlands, for instance, to be protected from the harsh summer sun. Noise is a problem for all breeds as they sleep on average twice as long in the day as humans — even guard dogs need their quiet rest. They must be protected against excessive noise, especially when eating or sleeping, so their kennel and yard should be situated in a quiet environment.

KING CHARLES SPANIELS (see page 60)

Dogs kept indoors also need their own permanent sleeping place and even though a well-trained even-tempered dog does not need to be closed in, it should have its own bed, preferably raised several inches above the floor to avoid draughts and the damp. A comfortably fitted-out cardboard box or shipping crate is a perfect place for a newly acquired puppy, where it will eat, sleep, and find a safe haven. The dog's bed and blankets should be regularly cleaned and if necessary disinfected as the dog may easily introduce into the home fleas and parasites from its encounters with other animals on the street. As well as their own sleeping place, dogs need to have their own dining areas where fresh drinking water is always available. If the dog is kept outside, the bowls that it eats and drinks from should be protected from falling rain, leaves, and dust.

A general principle to remember at all times when considering housing for dogs is that in their natural state they are pack animals. One of the worst forms of cruelty to a dog is to leave it alone in a kennel — even if it is taken out a couple of times a day for a walk. A dog needs constant social contact and it can never attain a state of well being if it is deprived of contact from people, other dogs, or animals that increase its experiences of the world.

The training of the puppy should start immediately, with the first essential being the dog's recognition of its own name, closely followed by the meaning of simple commands such as "come," "wait," and "no." This is really a matter of common sense; constant repetition of the puppy's name will ensure it quickly recognizes it, while praise and gentle admonishment will soon teach the puppy right from wrong. There is no short cut to house training a dog but from day one it should never be allowed to defecate or urinate in the house. A very young puppy should be taken outside as soon as it wakes and immediately after meals. At first this will be very frequent but as it learns to control its bladder the necessity for outside visits will decrease.

Puppies should be introduced as soon as possible to a soft leather collar and a leash. These are essential and the puppy must quickly learn to wear its collar and walk on the lead (a long lead affords the dog more freedom). Dogs should be taught to walk by their master's heel and, on the command "down," should sit comfortably, maintaining an alert air, neither lolling nor lying unconcernedly. A choke chain can be utilized for disobedient or hard to manage dogs. Some breeds, or dogs with a sensitive neck, do not take too kindly to a collar and in these cases a harness can be utilized. (Harnesses are also used with a variety of working dogs; there is a tracing type for police dogs, a draught type for sledge dogs, and a specially devised harness for guide dogs to the blind.)

Bringing a new puppy into the home requires a great deal of care and preparation. The daily care of a dog requires certain essential equipment including a brush, a curry comb for cleaning and combing the dog's coat, a trimming knife or scissors for rough-coated animals, towels for muddy paws and baths, and other aids depending on the breed. Grooming is not solely for the dog's appearance — it is essential for the dog's health. External parasites carried on the dog's coat transmit various internal diseases as well as mite and flea-born conditions. Vets can design an immunization program for any dog and recommend protection against infectious diseases and ailments, the most common ones being:

Canine Distemper
Symptoms: Begins with signs of respiratory problems and can attack any system.
Cause: A virus passed between dogs.
Cure: Preventative vaccines exist and must be administered yearly. Recovery is rare from a virus that attacks the nervous system.

Canine Hepatitis
Symptoms: Fever.
Cause: Viral disease.
Cure: Immunization.

Fleas
Symptoms: Itching, irritated skin.
Cause: Fleas in a dog's coat cause irritations or allergies.
Cure: Application of Insect Growth Control Regulators (IGR), non-toxic sterilizers that kill adult fleas.

Gastric Torsion
Symptoms: Gas, bloat, attempted vomiting.
Cause: Build up of gas that dilates and twists the stomach. Possible displacement of spleen and other organs.
Cure: Prompt surgery required. Dogs with large stomach cavities are thought to be most prone.
Monitor water intake, avoid feeding soy products, feed small meals, and encourage rest after feeding.

Heartworm Disease
Symptoms: Difficulty in breathing, swelling, collapse after slight exertion.
Cause: Worms infect heart and major blood vessels causing the disease. The infection is commonly spread by mosquitoes.
Cure: Administer larvicides; though not without a blood test.

Parvo or Corona Virus
Symptoms: Vomiting, fever, diarrhea.
Cause: Inflammation of the stomach or bowel (Gastroenteritis) caused by Parvo or Corona Virus.
Cure: Replace lost fluids, control nausea and diarrhea.
Parvo Virus is usually fatal though yearly vaccination can prevent it.
Contact with infected feces spreads the infection so watch your dog carefully.

Tapeworm
Symptoms: Bad coat, weight loss.
Cause: One type of worm is transmitted by fleas, another by rabbits.
Cure: Prevent dog from eating game and treat with effective medication.

MAREMMA SHEEPDOGS. This ancient breed has been used for 2,000 years to guard flocks of sheep from attack by wolves and bears.

Ticks
Symptoms: Fever, nasal, and eye discharge, loss of appetite.
Cause: Ticks attatch themselves to the skin, transmitting infections such as Lyme Disease and Ehrlichiosis.
Cure: After walks in areas that may be infested, check the coat for ticks and remove them.

Whip, Hook, Round Worms (Ascarid)
Symptoms: Bad stools, thin coats (Whip Worms).
Cause: Worms in the dog's gut.
Cure: Regular stool examinations help to control as does removal of feces so that dogs do not come into contact with it.

The amount of care that has to be devoted to the coat of the dog will obviously vary hugely according to the inherent nature of the breed. Most dogs do not need frequent bathing and some of the wire-haired breeds should not be bathed at all. Special shampoos are available for dogs and, as a general rule after bathing, the dog's coat should be allowed to dry naturally.

Bad breath is another common problem with dogs and can be caused by the animal's diet, tartar deposits on teeth, or by digestive problems. To help reduce plaque, feed your dog dry food and brush your dog's teeth once or twice a week with a toothbrush and dog toothpaste or moistened gauze pad — *never* use human toothpaste.

Most breeders will recommend a feeding program for the puppies they sell and this diet should be adhered to for at least the first couple of weeks. Good commercial puppy diets offer easily digested protein that contains the ten essential amino acids (see opposite). The quantities of food necessary for a healthy dog depends on the size of the breed but they must all be fed regularly with good quality fresh food. It is important to remember that a dog's food belongs in its bowl and should always be given in the same place at the same time and, if you have more than one dog, make sure each dog has its own food and water bowl. Rewards of biscuits or chocolates for special performances can be given by hand but, generally, feeding the dog by hand will spoil it. Any unconsumed food should be removed from the bowl to prevent the decaying material attracting flies or even rodents.

Don't leave your dog's food out longer than 30 minutes, if your dog has walked away from its bowl, it has probably had enough to eat.

Although a dog will eat just about anything, a well balanced diet containing plenty of animal protein is essential for its overall health. Just like humans, it is unhealthy for a dog to be overweight as excess weight endangers the heart, lungs, and joints and makes a dog more susceptible to other ailments. As a general guide, 16 percent meat mixed with vegetables and fiber (oat flakes, groats, rice, or the like) will give the animal its required nutrients. There are really seven basic ingredients that must be incorporated to give a completely balanced diet.

1. Protein, which must include the ten essential amino acids that the canine digestive system can synthesize. High quality protein can be found in fresh meat and fish.
2. Fat, which must contain all the necessary fatty acids. Fat should not exceed five percent of the diet.
3. Carbohydrates, in the form of biscuits, dog meal, toast, etc. should provide most of the diet's calorific requirement — protein and fat provides the rest.
4. Vitamins should be provided in supplements; especially for puppies, working dogs, stud dogs, and lactating bitches. Vital minerals and vitamins can be obtained with good-quality tinned dog food. Some poor quality dog foods contain meat products such as tendon, poultry heads, feet, and necks, which

MASTIFF (see page 99)

The LOWCHEN is native to France and is a member of the Bichon family (see page 44).

provide low-quality protein not easily digested by a dog.

5. Minerals are provided in good quality tinned foods and in tablets or other supplements with the advice of a vet.

6. Fiber does not provide any nutrients but is essential to help regulate healthy bowel movement. Beet pulp, a waste product of the sugar industry, is an ideal source of fiber because it provides no calories. A healthy canine diet should include about four percent fiber.

7. Water is the most important element of the diet (puppies should be given plenty of clean water, as nutritionists do not recommend milk after weaning).

A diet including all the necessary nutrients is essential but a dog's response to its food is also important because, as with humans, every dog has individual likes and dislikes. When presented with two varieties of equally nutritious foods a dog will naturally make a choice showing a clear preference for one over the other. Dogs will generally prefer meat to vegetable protein and will display a choice for type of meat. They will also respond to the way the food is offered; preferring canned or semi-moist food to dry food, cooked meat to raw meat, and, generally, canned meat to the same meat freshly cooked. Palatability plays a major role in a dog's food preference although the extent to which dogs are able to select their own food and when to eat it very much depends on their owner.

An irregular eating schedule can affect your dog's digestive system and ultimately cause chronic digestive disorders. Digestive problems can usually be improved by a change in diet. As obesity decreases a dog's life expectancy, maintaining a good balance between exercise and diet becomes more important as the dog ages. As the dog grows, exercise will improve its physical and mental health, but it is important to establish a regime which is compatible to both dog and owner. The dog's age, health, condition, and current activity level must be taken into consideration and, if in doubt, check with a vet before beginning anything vigorous. Dogs can't speak to tell when they have had enough so if it begins to pant too rapidly, *stop* exercising. Dogs can suffer from heat stroke, so you need to make sure your dog is not overexerting itself. Letting a dog play in the yard or garden doesn't qualify as exercise no matter how much it is encouraged to retrieve a stick or ball etc.

It is advisable that a vet should always be consulted to discuss the appropriate diet and fitness plan for a dog. But it is worth keeping in mind that:

- Puppies eat more and are highly active.
- Adult dogs have normal routines and food intake.
- Older dogs might require special diets and limited exercise.

With the training of dogs, owners must be aware of the different breeds and their inherent characteristics and realize that each breed should be treated and trained according to their nature. A great deal of care needs to be exercised and the owner will, in some cases, have to give up a lot of free time — training a dog is a long and often arduous process. There are no hard and fast rules in training; apart from breed characteristics, dogs are individuals and even puppies from the same litter can show marked personality differences. A good owner or trainer will avoid punishing a dog (except in the extreme instances of the dog attacking its owner, other people, or dogs) and will rely on verbal reproof for discipline. A dog that is scared of its owner or has no confidence in him will not make a good subject to train.

Obedience is the main thing a dog has to learn and it will usually be a willing subject as in its natural state it is a gregarious animal that will pursue the aim of reaching the highest possible status in its pack. To the modern dog its family is its pack, and if this family dotes on the animal and is weak with discipline the animal will take advantage and become a pest to everybody concerned. A puppy must be taught that it comes at the bottom of the pack in the hierarchy of its new family. The owner has to firmly establish himself as the leader of the pack, yet supply all the dog's needs with understanding and care — then he will have a loving and loyal companion for life.

Should a dog ever need to be punished, the admonishment should come immediately after the misdeed so the animal is completely aware of why it is being punished. The owner should never lose his temper with his pet or force it to do things that the dog is unhappy about. To successfully control an animal, the human owner must be in control of themself; a nervous owner will result in a nervous dog. Dogs should never be shouted at, struck, nor have their heads threatened.

Training a dog is not solely for work or show purposes as an untrained dog, in some circumstances, can be an extremely dangerous dog. In the UK for instance, many breeds are now required by law to wear a muzzle when in public. Being a good citizen applies to the owners as well as their dogs particularly in public places. An owner who considers other people when walking their dogs is showing consideration.

Owners who believe that training a dog is somehow unnatural or even cruel should realize that training is not a nuisance to the dog but is actually necessary for the animal's own safety. It is fun for the dog and gives it a chance to demonstrate its abilities, especially in the company of other dogs. It must be obvious to all the danger that an untrained dog presents to itself, other people, and other dogs if left to roam the streets unattended, or the danger to livestock should it be free in the countryside.

The first 16 weeks of a dog's life is when its socialization between humans and other dogs takes place and will set the pattern for its next 12 or so years with a well brought up dog displaying loyalty, and giving great pleasure and companionship to its owner.

For a new pedigree dog owner who wants to show their dog, the initial stage is to join a dog club which holds classes that teach the basics of handling a dog. Dog clubs are involved in many activities besides putting on a dog show and will generally welcome new members. The shows that local dog clubs organize are for fun and are used for practice and the training of both dogs and novice exhibitors. While these shows award no points they are a good place to start before entering the "serious" business of real shows. There are all types of dog show — they are not limited to shows that merely exhibit the appearance and true-to-breed characteristics of a dog. Specialist shows will, for example, allow a Beagle to exhibit its tracking abilities or a Weimaraner its hunting skills.

In hunting tests, the dog's ability to perform is judged against a standard of perfection established by the national Kennel Club rules in whichever country the trials are held. In field trials, the dogs compete against each other for placements and points toward their championships. These field events are usually divided by subgroups of dogs — Spaniels, Retrievers, etc. — but are sometimes limited to specific breeds. Herding breeds such as Collies or the German Shepherd (Alsation), have their own trials and tests that are designed to allow a dog to demonstrate its ability to herd livestock under the direction of a handler. Dogs are judged against a set of standards and can earn advanced titles and championships in the trials, where they compete not only against a standard, but against other dogs for placements. Stock used at the trials can be sheep, cattle, goats, or even ducks.

Owners of Sighthounds may be interested in the "coursing" competitions in which dogs follow an artificial lure around a course on an open field and are scored on speed, enthusiasm, agility, endurance, and their ability to follow the lure. These events help to keep a hound physically and mentally fit too. There are also so-called Earth Dog trials for the smaller terriers that were originally bred to "go-to-ground" after quarry, which ranged from rats to badgers. The object of the test is to give the dog an opportunity to display its ability to follow game and "work," that is show interest by barking, digging, and scratching the quarry.

A proud owner of a purebred dog probably knows that written references to the history of his Beagle can be found as far back as Chaucer in the 14th century, that his Saluki, "The Royal Dog of Egypt," is arguably the oldest known breed of domestic dog, or that his Pomeranian is descended from the sled dogs of Iceland and Lapland. Every breed of dog has its own rich and colorful history

The WELSH COLLIE is a member of the collie family (see page 65).

and most Kennel Clubs worldwide will have events that will be challenging and exciting for an owner and his dog. These events provide an opportunity for dogs to work with their owners to perform the functions for which the breed was developed and receive recognition for achievement in the form of ribbons, trophies, and titles.

For whatever reason a dog is purchased, to guard the home, to work in the field, to be shown, or just to be there as a faithful and loving companion, the responsibility of the owner towards the animal can never be underestimated. Anyone buying a dog must be prepared to understand that the animal has its own feelings, needs, and perceptions, yet will be entirely dependent on them — the owner. The pet should be bought from a reputable breeder and everything needed for its well being should have been provided before the little animal is brought into the home. It is not just a matter of material provisions, the owner has to learn to adapt to the dog's needs and acquire desirable ownership traits. The responsibilities of the owner extend beyond the dog itself, to their duties towards neighbors and the other people around their pet — their dog should always be under control. Apart from the nuisance that an untrained dog can cause, an unhealthy dog can transmit diseases to other animals and people so it must be kept in tip-top medical condition. Nothing can justify cruelty to animals, so it may be better to have an unwanted pet painlessly put down than given away without knowing what care any new owner will provide.

This being said, there is no doubt about the importance of pets in a person's life. Dogs have played a significant role down the ages and continue to provide a constant source of joy. Today the importance of working dogs such as sheep dogs or guard dogs is diminishing, and these wonderful animals are increasingly becoming purely pets. They are invaluable companions for the old, the lonely, the blind, and as part of a human "pack" bring great joy to the whole family — truly a "man's best friend."

DOG BREEDS

Affenpinscher

TOY GROUP: USA & UK

Origin: From Germany, this is one of the oldest toy dogs dating back to the 17th century, although there is only a small amount of information available as it is a rare breed. Initially used as a ratter in stables, the dog was originally bigger than the one we know today and was black, reddish black, or salt and pepper in color. Some sources suggest that the present conformation is due to a man living near Lübeck in Germany who concentrated on producing a smaller breed to be used as a mouser in the home.

Size & Substance: Height: 9-11.5in. Weight: 6lb 7oz-9lb.
This is a sturdy, compact breed, with medium bone.

Colors: Black, black and tan, silver-gray, red.

Coat: The Affenpinscher's coat should be dense, rough, and harsh textured.

Temperament: The Affenpinscher is loyal and affectionate toward its owner and friends but is watchful of strangers and completely fearless toward aggressors. With its monkey-like appearance, it is sometimes referred to as the "Black Devil" and its lively character and antics make it an excellent and entertaining companion.

Afghan Hound

HOUND GROUP: USA & UK

Origin: This is one of the typical Sighthounds or "gaze hounds" of the world and, as its name implies, it originates from the mountains of Afghanistan where it was an extraordinarily agile hunter. It is generally agreed that the Afghan and the Saluki are descended from the same source, but which came first is an argument that will probably never be resolved.

The Afghan was unknown in the Western world until the late 19th century when members of the British Army took specimens home to breed. Much of the modern history of the breed is due to the work of Major Amps and his wife who returned to England from Afghanistan with their stock of Afghans after World War I.

Today the Afghan Hound is best known as a glamorous show dog.

Size and Substance: Height: dogs 27-29in; bitches 25-27in.
This breed must not be heavily bodied and hipbones should be prominent.

Colors: Any solid color is acceptable, including black and tan or domino (a dark coat on the saddle and face with pale leg furnishings and top-knot).

Coat: Naturally developed with a long and very fine texture on the body.

Temperament: The Afghan Hound is a dignified and aloof dog with a certain eager fierceness.

Airedale Terrier

TERRIER GROUP: USA & UK

Origin: The Airedale Terrier, the largest of the terrier breeds, was one of the first breeds utilized by the police in Great Britain and Germany. The majority of terriers were primarily introduced by workers in the wool industry and miners of the West Riding of Yorkshire in the small villages along the Aire and Whafe rivers and the dog originally had various appellations. However, in 1882, the breed became known, by popular acclaim, as the Airedale Terrier.

The Airedale's prowess as a surface and waterside hunter no doubt owes its inception to the passion for otter hunting of the residents of this region. This very versatile breed was also used during World War II as a guard, for messenger duty, and for rodent control, but today this "king of terriers" is just as much at ease in town or country although it requires space and regular exercise.

Size & Substance: Height from top of shoulder: dogs 23-24in; bitches 22-23in.
Sturdy, well muscled and boned, the Airedale gives the impression of great strength and substance.

Colors: Black body, top of neck, and top surface of tail. All other parts tan. A red mixture is often found in the black and is acceptable. A small white blaze on the chest is a characteristic of certain strains of the breed.

Coat: Dense and wiry lying straight and close with a shorter, softer undercoat.

Temperament: The Airedale Terrier is confident, outgoing, friendly, courageous, and intelligent.

Akita/Japanese Akita

WORKING GROUP: USA/UTILITY GROUP: UK

Origin: This large, upstanding, dignified Spitz is the most popular breed in its native Japan where it takes its name from the prefecture of Akita in the north of the country. The Akita can be traced back some three hundred years and today's dog, with its distinctive tail and ears, resembles the dog found carved on early Japanese tombs. In 1931, the Japanese government designated the Akita as a National Monument and as one of the country's national treasures.

It is the largest of any breed surviving in Japan today and was originally a hunter of bear, deer, and wild boar.

Size & Substance: Height at withers: dogs 26-28in; bitches 24-26in.
The most obvious physical characteristic of this breed is its heavy bone structure.

Colors: The Akita can be any color including white, brindle, or pinto and its coloration is brilliant and clear. Markings are well defined, with or without a mask or blaze.

Coat: A coarse and straight outercoat stands off body and there is a soft, thick, and wooly undercoat. The coat at the withers and rump is slightly longer than the rest of body, except on the tail where it is more profuse. There should be no indication of a ruff or feathering.

Temperament: The Akita is dignified and courageous with a tendency to dominate other dogs. It is intelligent but needs to be trained by an experienced trainer as it has a tendency to show aggression towards other dogs.

Alaskan Malamute

WORKING GROUP: USA & UK

Origin: The use of dogs as working animals has been part of the culture of peoples from the Arctic regions since the Stone Age. This "tractor of the north" takes its name from the Mahlemut settlement of Inuits hailing from the rugged western area of Alaska and bears a close resemblance to the Husky. It is the most powerful of the sledge dogs and had to be hardy to stay alive in its original environment, where its main task was to pull heavily laden sledges in extreme weather conditions.

European explorers and Russian whalers used to tell of the Mahlemut tribes' beautiful dogs and they became much sought after by the foreigners who settled in Alaska.

Size & Substance: Height: dogs 25-28in; bitches 23-26in. Weight: 85-125lb.
This dog should have heavy bones and a well-knit body.

Colors: The coloration of this breed ranges from light gray, through intermediate shadings, to black; or from gold, through shades of red, to liver. However, it is always white on the underbody, parts of its legs and feet, and a part of its mask marking. Markings are either cap-like or mask-like on the face and a white blaze on the forehead is permissible. A heavy mantling of unbroken color is also acceptable. The only solid color permissible is all white.

Coat: A thick and coarse guard coat protects a dense, oily, and wooly undercoat. The guard coat stands out with especially thick fur round the neck. The Malamute's coat renders it immune to low temperatures and it will happily curl up and go to sleep in a snow blizzard.

Temperament: Affectionate, loyal, and friendly, the Alaskan Malamute is family orientated and loves to be with people.

Australian Cattle Dog

HERDING GROUP: USA/ WORKING GROUP: UK

Origin: A medium-sized dog greatly prized for its working ability in its native Australia, where it was bred to support the establishment of the cattle industry and is used for the control and herding of cattle in all environments. With the high temperatures and long distances in Australia, the principal requirement for a cattle dog was exceptional resilience and stamina.

Early breeders kept precious few records of their dogs but it is generally agreed that the breed resulted from the crossing of Smooth Collies with the dingo, with the later injection of Dalmatian and black and tan Kelpie blood. Its habit of crouching low behind cattle and controlling them by nipping at their heels has given it the sobriquet "Australian Heeler" in some parts of the world.

Size & Substance: Height at withers: dogs 18-20in; bitches 17-19in. A good specimen of this breed has a correct balance between skeletal structure and structural relationships.

Colors: This breed can be either blue or red. Blue should be mottled or blue speckled, with or without other markings; while if red, the coat should show a good even red speckle all over (including the undercoat) with or without darker red markings on head.

Coat: A smooth, weather resistant outercoat lies over a short, dense undercoat.

Temperament: This breed is alert, intelligent, courageous, trustworthy, and devoted to its work. While it is naturally suspicious of strangers as it diligently protects its herdsman, stock, and property, its devotion to duty means it is biddable and amenable to handling.

Australian Terrier

TERRIER GROUP: USA & UK

Origin: This small dog, originally from Australia, where it is very popular, is said to include many of the terrier breeds that were undoubtedly derived from stock that was British in origin. It was essentially bred as a working terrier where its watchfulness and vociferous nature were utilized to guard mines and tend sheep.

First known as the Broken-haired Terrier, perhaps its greatest skill is as an extremely effective hunter and dispatcher of vermin. The breed was officially recognized by the British Kennel Club in 1933, but it was not until 1960 that it gained AKC recognition.

Size & Substance: Height at withers: 10in. Weight: 14lb.
This is a small, well-balanced, well-muscled dog.

Colors: The Heeler should be blue, steel blue, or dark gray blue with rich tan markings on face, ears, under body, lower legs, and feet. A blue or silver "top-knot" of a lighter shade than the head color is common among the breed. However, a clear sandy or red coat with a "top-knot" of a lighter shade is also seen and is quite permissible.

Coat: The Australian Terrier has a harsh, straight, dense, and weather-resistant top coat with short, soft textured undercoat. The muzzle, lower legs and feet are free from long hair.

Temperament: The "Aussie" is tough, friendly, extrovert, obedient, and eager to please, with the courage of a much larger dog.

Basenji

HOUND GROUP: USA & UK

Origin: It has been the subject of much conjecture that this hound of great antiquity was a palace dog of the Pharaohs of ancient Egypt — the paintings of the dogs in their tombs certainly bear a striking resemblance to their modern counterparts. British explorers in the African Congo sighted these dogs in the 17th century and they were subsequently imported to Britain. Today, the breed has been maintained in its purest form on the British island of Malta. Because of the strange throaty crowing noise it makes it has been labeled the "barkless dog" and is remarkable for its almost cat-like cleanliness.

Size & Substance: Height at withers: dogs 17in; bitches 16in. Weight: dogs 24lb; bitches 21lb.
The dog should appear well balanced.

Colors: Combinations that commonly occur in this breed are, pure black and white; red and white; black, tan, and white; black, tan, and white with tan melon pips and mask. Ideally the white should be on the feet, chest, and tail tip.

Coat: This should be very fine and short, sleek, and close.

Temperament: The Basenji is an intelligent, independent, alert, and affectionate dog, though it has a tendency to be aloof with strangers.

Bassett Hound

HOUND GROUP: USA & UK

Origin: Of all the dog breeds in the world this is perhaps the one most commonly depicted as the affable but worried clown, and with its placid nature it richly deserves its popularity as a family dog.

The forerunners of the Basset Hound first appeared in 16th century France where the French word *basset* means low-set. They originally assumed a curiosity value when they appeared in litters of French staghounds. During the evolutionary process many types of Basset emerged, but the modern Bassets can be traced to the Basset D'Artoise and the Basset Normand.

Size & Substance: Height at withers: 13-15in.
This is a strong boned breed, with great substance. It should be relatively low to the ground with a moderate length of body.

Colors: The Basset is most commonly black, white, and tan (tri-color) or lemon and white (bicolor). However, any recognized hound colors are acceptable.

Coat: This is smooth, short, and close without being too fine.

Temperament: Generally placid and affectionate, if sometimes a little stubborn, the Basset Hound is neither aggressive or timid. This indomitable "Hush-Puppy" is quite content to lie in front of the blazing hearth, but naturally, as a tenacious hound of ancient lineage, it is equally happy on the heath, doggedly pursuing its natural prey, the hare, over prodigious distances. The short-legged Basset, with its domed head and wrinkled brow, has an expression of calm and almost comic seriousness and its deep, resounding bark somewhat belies the truth of its extremely friendly nature that can be verified by the multitude of fans it has worldwide.

Beagle

HOUND GROUP: USA & UK

Origin: The Beagle is the smallest of the scenthounds, and originates from the British Isles, where it hunted rabbit and hare in packs, with the huntsmen following on foot. Written references to the breed can be found as far back as Chaucer in the 14th century.

With the decline of hunting in the United Kingdom since the 1950s, many breeds of coursers have almost disappeared and today are kept mainly as pets. But, in recent years, the American Beagle has contributed significantly to the progress of its British counterpart with a number of quality stud dogs crossing eastwards across the Atlantic. As a result of this, since the 1970s, the breed has produced many Group and Best in Show winners in the UK.

Size & Substance: The USA has two varieties. Height at withers of the first: 13 in; and the second: 13-15 in. UK Height: 13-16 in.
A miniature Foxhound, the Beagle is solid and big for his inches.

Colors: Blanketed tri-color is the most popular coloration, but any recognized hound colors other than liver are acceptable. The tip of the tail is traditionally white.

Coat: This should be a typical hound coat — short, dense, and weatherproof.

Temperament: The Beagle is alert, amiable, and eager, showing no aggression or timidity. Although it has that wear-and-tear look of the hound that can last in the chase and follow its quarry to the death, its quiet and even-tempered nature makes it an ideal family dog.

Bearded Collie

HERDING GROUP: USA/WORKING GROUP: UK

Origin: This is one of Britain's oldest breeds and for centuries was bred as a companion and servant of man, but it wasn't until 1967 that the first litter of Bearded Collies was born in the United States.

It has been conjectured that during the 16th century, when Scotland was involved in trading with Poland, Polish sailors may have traded their Polski Owczarek Nizinny dogs for valuable sheep. The Polish dogs mixed with the Highland Collies and later became what is now known as the Bearded Collie.

Size & Substance: Height: dogs 21-22 in; bitches 20-21in.

Colors: There are many accepted variations of color for the Bearded Collie. Slate gray, reddish-fawn, black, blue, all shades of gray, brown, and sandy can appear with or without white markings. Where white does occur, it may appear on the foreface as a blaze, as well as on the skull, the tip of the tail, the chest, legs and feet, and around the neck.

Coat: The outercoat of a Bearded Collie is flat, harsh, strong, and shaggy — it is free from wooliness and curl, although a slight wave is permissible. The undercoat is soft, furry, and close.

Temperament: An easy-going, intelligent working dog with no nervousness or aggression, the "Beardie" is ideally suited to life in the country where its ancestors drove cattle and sheep to market through the windswept hills and glens of Scotland. This wonderful breed makes an excellent family dog for those who have enough space to keep it happy and healthy.

Bedlington Terrier

TERRIER GROUP: USA & UK

Origin: This strong, lithe, and graceful terrier, originally bred in England for hunting, was first known as the Rothbury, Rodbury, or Northumberland Fox Terrier in its native Northumberland. The first dog known as a Bedlington Terrier was owned by Joseph Ainsley of Bedlington. Its original purpose of going to ground to catch vermin changed over time, and it was later used to catch rabbits on the ground; consequently, it developed a more rugged frame with longer legs.

The breed's unique appearance, combined with its assertive demeanor are two reasons why it is described as having "the head of a lamb," and "the heart of a lion."

Size & Substance: Height at withers: dogs 16.5in; bitches 15.5in. Weight: 18-23lb, proportionate to height. Ideally, the Bedlington terrier is a muscular and markedly flexible dog.

Colors: Permissible colors are blue, liver, or sandy, and can be with or without tan markings. In bicolors, the tan markings are found on the legs, chest, under the tail, inside the hindquarters, and over each eye. The "topknots" of all adults should be lighter than the body color. Darker body pigmentation of all colors is to be encouraged.

Coat: This breed has a thick and linty (not wiry) coat, which stands well out from the skin.

Temperament: The Bedlington Terrier is even tempered with an affectionate nature quite suitable for family life. It is mild by nature but full of courage when aroused.

Belgian Shepherd Dogs

HERDING GROUP: USA/WORKING GROUP: UK

Origin: In 1891, the breed known throughout the world as the Belgian Shepherd Dog was officially created consisting of four varieties named for an area in Belgium where they were developed and most prized: the Groenendael, the Laekenois, the Malinois, and the Tervueren. Today, the status of one breed of Belgian Shepherd Dog with four varieties is accepted by the Fédération Cynologique Internationale (FCI) and most kennel clubs, but in the USA, the Groenendael is designated as the Belgian Sheepdog by the AKC which doesn't recognize the wire-haired Laekenois.

Size & Substance: Height at withers: dogs 24-26in; bitches 22-24in.
The bone structure of all the varieties should be moderately heavy in proportion to the dog's height so that it is well balanced throughout.

Colors: This breed is generally black, or black with white, limited as follows: a small to moderate patch or strip may appear on the forechest, between the pads of the feet, on the tips of hind toes, and on chin and muzzle (this frost may be either white or gray).

GROENENDAEL

Coat: A long, medium harsh, well fitting, straight, and abundant coat is desirable and should be neither silky nor wiry. The dog will also have an extremely dense undercoat commensurate with climatic conditions.

Temperament: All the varieties of the Belgian Shepherd Dog are affectionate, intelligent, courageous, and friendly. Possessive of their family, they will need a great deal of attention from their owners.

Groenendael/Chien de Berger Belge: During World War I, these well balanced and elegant dogs distinguished themselves on the battlefields of Europe, serving as message carriers, ambulance dogs, and even pulling machine guns.

Tervueren: This variety owes its name to the Belgian village of Tervueren and was created after World War II from the longhaired puppies in Malinois litters and the fawn-gray puppies in Groenendael litters. Prior to 1959, the Belgian Tervurens were registered and shown as Belgian Sheepdogs. In that year however, the AKC granted them separate classification designating the Belgian Tervuren as a distinct breed.

Malinois: The Belgian Malinois was bred around the city of Malines from whence the name is derived.

Laekenois: This reddish-fawn dog, with its short, wiry coat, is the rarest variety of the Belgian Shepherd Dogs in the UK. It is not recognized as a separate breed in the USA.

Bernese Mountain Dog

WORKING GROUP: USA & UK

Origin: This breed's ancestors are thought to have been first found in Switzerland more than 2,000 years ago. Roman soldiers brought Caesar's Mastiffs, utilized as guard dogs, to the region, and these were crossed with the native flock-guarding dogs.

This large, strong, tricolored dog is known in its native Switzerland as the Berner Sennenhund, which literally translated means Bernese Alpine herdsmen's dog. They have historically worked as cattle drovers, draft dogs pulling cheese and milk carts, and watchdogs in the mountainous farmlands of the canton of Berne.

Size & Substance: Height at withers: dogs 25-27.5in; bitches 23-26in. Sturdy bone is of great importance in this breed.

Colors: The Bernese Mountain Dog is tricolored; it has a jet-black coat with reddish-brown markings on its legs, cheeks, and above the eyes. Clear white, symmetrical spots on the head and chest, white paws, and a white tail tip are much to be desired.

Coat: This should be thick, soft, silky, glossy, long, and slightly wavy, though it should not curl.

Temperament: Wary but neither timid, nervous, nor aggressive, the Bernese Mountain Dog is self-confident, alert, and good-natured. It makes a faithful and devoted friend though it may remain aloof to the attentions of strangers. Because the dog was originally bred to withstand the severe weather conditions sometimes encountered in the Alps it, not surprisingly, does not do very well in hot or humid conditions.

Bichon Frisé

NON-SPORTING GROUP: USA/ TOY GROUP: UK

Origin: The Bichon Frisé, whose name translates as "fluffy little dog," originated in the Mediterranean area. Its true history is, however, relatively unknown though there is a widespread belief that a small, coated dog, often white, existed before the time of Christ. The sturdy, white, powder puff of a dog that we know today was bred to be a lap dog for French royalty. You can even find Bichons Frisé portrayed in some of the paintings by the classical Spanish artist Goya. However, during the French Revolution they became street dogs and only the toughest survived.

Size & Substance: Height at withers: 9-11in.
This breed is compact and of medium bone.

Colors: White is the most common color, but it may have very limited shadings of buff, cream, or apricot around the ears or on the body.

Coat: The Bichon Frisé coat is fine and silky with soft corkscrew curls and a soft, dense undercoat. It is neither flat nor corded. The texture of the coat is of utmost importance in this breed and when bathed and brushed, it stands off the body, creating an overall powder puff appearance.

Temperament:
Outgoing, gentle, sensitive, and friendly, a cheerful attitude is the "hallmark" of the Bichon Frisé breed.

Bloodhound

HOUND GROUP; USA &UK

Origin: The Bloodhound is an extremely old breed and was alive and thriving in Greece long before the coming of Christianity. The modern Bloodhound has its origins in the Ardenne region of central Europe on the French — Belgian border. It was in this region that the large game hounds of St Hubert and Talbot and the white Southern Hound were crossed to produce the dog known as the Chien de St Hubert. Even today in some countries the terms Bloodhound and Chien de St Hubert are interchangeable.

The Bloodhound possesses, in a most marked degree, the characteristics of "Sagaces" (dogs which hunt together by scent), the luxuriant wrinkles about its head and neck entrap the scent of the target. The first recorded use of Bloodhounds by organized law enforcement was in England in 1805, when they were utilized to search for poachers and thieves. Even today, testimony of a Bloodhound's man trailing results is acceptable in almost any court. The breed's amazing abilities have given them an almost super-canine reputation that has been perpetuated by the writers of crime thrillers.

Size & Substance: Height: dogs 26in; bitches 24in. Weight: dogs 90lb; bitches 80lb.

Colors: Black and tan, liver and tan, or red are the accepted colors for this breed. The darker colors are sometimes interspersed with lighter or badger-colored hair, and sometimes flecked with white. A small amount of white is permissible on the chest, feet, and tip of stern.

Coat: This is short, smooth, and weatherproof as is typical of the Hound group.

Temperament: The Bloodhound is somewhat reserved and sensitive, though affectionate. It relates well to other dogs.

Border Collie

HERDING GROUP: USA/WORKING GROUP: UK

Origin: The Border Collie is derived from various breeds including Bearded Collies, Harlequins, Bob-tailed Sheepdogs, and Smithfields. Intelligence is the hallmark of the breed and its energy, alertness, and eagerness have made it the world's premier sheep herding dog.

The border referred to in its name is the English-Scottish one, the area where the breed originally evolved and was utilized to work sheep. Capable of thinking for itself, the Border Collie has often been employed in mountain rescue work and makes an admirable tracker dog.

Size & Substance: Height at withers: dogs 19-22in; bitches 18-21in. Overall balance between height, length, weight, and bone is crucial and is more important than any absolute measurement.

Colors: A variety of colors are permissible, but white should never predominate. The most common color is black, with or without the traditional white blaze, collar, stockings, and tail tip, or the tan points that can also occur.

Coat: Two types of coat are common. The first is rough, which should be moderately long and flat or slightly wavy. The smooth coat is short over entire body. In both cases the topcoat is dense and medium textured and the puppies have a short, soft, dense, water-resistant coat that becomes the undercoat in adult dogs.

Temperament: The Border Collie is highly intelligent, keen, alert, and responsive. Neither aggressive nor nervous, it is affectionate towards friends but sensibly reserved towards strangers, making it an excellent watchdog. With a hard, muscular body giving it substance and stamina, this is one of the breeds that exemplifies the work ethic.

Border Terrier

TERRIER GROUP: USA & UK

Origin: Border Terriers were bred to hunt with Foxhounds in the countryside of the northeast of England. Today, all the world's kennel clubs recognize the breed and it is one of the top 20 most popular breeds in the UK.

Size & Substance: Height at withers: approx. 13in. Weight: dogs 13-15lb 7oz; bitches 11lb 7oz-14lb.
These are appropriate weights for Border Terriers in hardworking condition. The breed is characterized by medium bone and is strongly put together.

Colors: Permitted colors are red, wheaten, grizzle and tan, and blue and tan. A small amount of white is also permitted and a dark muzzle is characteristic and highly desirable.

Coat: The Border Terrier has a weather-resistant, harsh, and dense coat with a close, soft undercoat.

Temperament: This active, tough, and hard-bitten breed, perfectly exemplifies the qualities of a terrier. It has a characteristic "otter" head with a keen eye, and with its strong body, endurance, and agility it is renowned for fearlessness and determined resolve. By nature, in the field, The Border Terrier is "hard as nails" — as "game as they come," but as a family companion it is good-tempered, affectionate, obedient, and easily trained.

Borzoi

HOUND GROUP: USA & UK

Origin: The Borzoi, once known as the Russian Wolfhound, originated in 17th century Russia, when Arabian Greyhounds were crossed with a thick-coated Russian breed — its name means "swift" in its native country. This tall dog, sometimes referred to as "the king of hounds," relies on sight rather than scent, and was originally utilized as a coursing dog to hunt large game animals on more or less open terrain.

Size & Substance: UK Height at withers: dogs 29in; bitches 27in. USA: 26-28in. Weight: dogs 75-105lb; bitches 15-20lb less.
Sturdy bones are a prime characteristic of this breed.

Colors: Any color is acceptable.

Coat: Long, silky, flat, wavy, or rather curly, on the head, ears, and front of legs, the coat of the Borzoi should be short and smooth. On the neck, the frill should be profuse and rather curly while feathering on the hindquarters and tail is long and profuse.

Temperament: The Borzoi is sensitive, alert, and aloof. Although not as fast as some other hounds, it has incredible stamina and endurance and prospective owners should be advised that Borzois require vigorous exercise to keep them in fit condition. Due to their sighthound heritage, they should never be let off a leash or left to roam outside of a fenced yard.

Boston Terrier

NON-SPORTING GROUP: USA/UTILITY GROUP: UK

Origin: This dog, as its name suggests, is a breed native to America, originating in Boston, and is derived from crosses between the Bulldog and Terrier. The unique characteristics of the Boston Terrier have resulted in a most dapper and charming American original and this "Yankee Doodle Dandy" is sometimes referred to as "the American gentleman among dogs." It is one of a handful of breeds which has been developed in the United States.

Size & Substance:
Lightweight: Under 15lb.
Middleweight: 15-20lb.
Heavyweight: 21-25lb.
The length of leg must balance with the length of body to give the Boston Terrier its striking square appea-rance. Bone and muscle must be in proportion.

Colors: This breed can be black, brindle, or seal (seal appears black, but when viewed in the sun or bright light it has a red cast) with white markings, although brindle is preferred *only* if all other qualities are equal. Required markings are a white muzzle band, white blaze between the eyes, and a white forechest. Desired markings include a white muzzle band, an even white blaze between the eyes or over the head, a white collar, a white forechest, white on part or whole of the forelegs and hind legs below the hocks.

Coat: Short, smooth, and bright, the coat should be fine in texture.

Temperament: The Boston Terrier possesses an excellent disposition. A most important characteristic of the breed is it expression — the ideal Boston Terrier should convey an appearance that is alert and kind, indicating a high degree of intelligence. It is often a clown and its loving and sensitive nature, coupled with its deep love for its family and children, make it a perfect pet.

Bouvier des Flandres

HERDING GROUP: USA/WORKING GROUP: UK

Origin: As its name suggests, this powerfully built compact dog, originated in the Flanders area of Belgium where it has long been prized for its remarkable abilities as an all purpose farm dog. With a harsh coat to protect it in all weathers enabling it to perform the most arduous tasks, this breed has been utilized as a cattle driver, guardian, protector, and in modern times as an ambulance and messenger dog. Its physical and mental characteristics, coupled with its olfactory abilities, intelligence, and initiative, also see it used as a tracking dog and a guide dog for the blind.

Size & Substance: USA height: dogs up to 27.5in; bitches up to 26.5in. UK height: dogs 25-27in; bitches 23-25.5in. Weight: 75-95lb.

Powerfully built, strong boned, and well muscled, this dog has no sign of heaviness or clumsiness.

Colors: The coloration of the Bouvier des Flandres ranges from fawn, through to black, including brindle. A small white star on the chest is permitted.

Coat: This should be an abundant, coarse, weather-resistant with a soft and dense undercoat. The upper lip, with its heavy moustache, and the chin, with its heavy and rough beard, gives that gruff expression so characteristic of the breed.

Temperament: Sensible and calm, resolute and fearless, the Bouvier des Flandres is a dependable dog. Although the Bouvier is a natural guard dog it is not an attack dog but is a tolerant character and enjoys the company of children, making it a good family pet.

Boxer

WORKING GROUP: USA & UK

Origin: The Boxer is a working dog developed in Germany in the 1880s from several other breeds, including the Bulldog and Great Dane. It is so called because it strikes out with its front paws when it fights. Virtually all the leading Boxers in the world can trace their ancestry back to a single brindle and white bitch called "Meta von der Passage" (born in 1898).

The Boxer was originally developed to serve as guard, working, and companion dog and it combines strength and agility with elegance and style. Until recent times docking of the ears and tail of the Boxer was usual in Europe but in Britain this practice has largely been given up. Some argue that without their ears and tails docked Boxers lose their keen appearance but at least the puppies don't have to suffer these painful operations. The chiseled head imparts to the Boxer a unique individual stamp, with the broad, blunt muzzle the distinctive feature — this, added to the dog's proud bearing, gives it "nobility."

Size & Substance: Height at withers: dogs 22.5-25in; bitches 21-23in. Weight: dogs 66-70lb; bitches 55-60lb. Proper balance and quality in the individual should be of primary importance with the ideal Boxer being medium-sized, square built, and of good substance, with a short back and strong limbs.

Colors: Fawn or brindle with a black muzzle are the accepted colors with white markings not covering more than a third of the body surface being acceptable. Brindles must have black stripes on the base fawn color, with the stripes being in distinct relief.

Coat: Short, glossy, smooth, and tight to the body.

Temperament: Self-assured, alert, and fearless yet equitable and biddable, the Boxer is the ultimate "people dog," playful, good natured, and quick to learn. After careful training it makes a good family pet when given plenty of exercise.

Briard/Berger de Brie

HERDING GROUP: USA/WORKING GROUP: UK

Origin: The Briard, "a heart wrapped with fur," is a very old breed of French, rough-coated shepherd dogs, which retains a high degree of its ancestral instinct to guard home and master. The breed's history is said to trace back to the days of the Emperor Charlemagne, and French folklore relates many tales of its outstanding acts of courage and heroism.

The breed's ancestors were probably rough-coated sheepdogs brought into Europe in the Middle Ages accompanying warring Asian invaders. The first litter of Briards registered with the AKC was in 1922, but the breed only arrived in Britain, by way of Ireland, in the 1960s.

Size & Substance: Height at withers: dogs 24-27in; bitches 23-25.5in. Maximum weight: 66lb.
The Briard is strong in bone and muscle, exhibiting the strength and agility required of the typical herding dog.

Colors: All black or black with white hairs scattered through the coat are acceptable, as is fawn in all its shades. The Briard should not be all white. Combinations of two of these colors are permitted, provided there are no marked spots and the transition from one color to another takes place gradually and symmetrically.

Coat: This is coarse, hard, long, slightly wavy, and very dry with a fine dense undercoat. The coat is tight on all the body.

Temperament: The Briard is fearless, with no trace of aggressiveness. It is a dog with spirit and initiative, intelligent, easily trained, faithful, gentle, and obedient.

Brittany/Épagneul Breton

SPORTING GROUP: USA/GUNDOG GROUP: UK

Origin: The Bretons' slender dogs have been written about since as far back as AD 150 but the first accurate records are to be found in paintings and tapestries dating from the 17th century. The breed can be tailless or have a tail that is usually docked to approximately four inches; in theory, the first tailless Brittany was born in the mid-1800s.

Size & Substance: Height: 17.5-20.5in. Weight: 30- 40lb.

Colors: The Brittany can be orange and white, liver and white, black and white, or roan. Any of these colors, or tricolor (allowed but not preferred) is permitted. A tricolor is a liver and white dog with orange markings. Black is not allowed in the USA.

Coat: This is rather flat, dense, fairly fine, and slightly wavy, but neither wiry nor silky.

Temperament: Eager to please and affectionate, happy, and alert, these dogs usually have exceptionally friendly temperaments; they love people, albeit second to birds, and get along well with other dogs. This makes them excellent house dogs as long as the owner is prepared to operate on the same high energy level. This rugged breed, with its strength and agility, is a natural pointer and excellent retriever. It makes a great hunting companion and in the USA today, the Brittany is the most popular of all pointing breeds in the field.

Brussels Griffon

TOY GROUP: USA & UK

Origin: This was originally a rough street dog, often found killing rats in the stables of old Belgium, but has now made a smooth transition into what is often a life of luxury. The Stable Griffon (Griffon d'Ecurie) was bred with Affenpinschers and the blood of the Dutch Pug and the Ruby English Toy Spaniel was introduced to produce the Brussels Griffon of today.

Size & Substance: Weight: 6-10lb. Type and quality are of greater importance than weight and this breed should be thickset, well boned, and compact with good balance.

Colors: The Brussels Griffon can be red, black, or black and rich tan without white markings. Frosting on the whiskers of mature dogs is common and acceptable.

Coat: There are two varieties: roughs have a harsh, wiry, and dense coat that is free from curl and preferably with an undercoat: while the smooths have a short and tight, smooth and glossy coat with no trace of wiry hair.

Temperament: The first impressions when encountering a Griff are its overwhelming personality, full of self-importance, and a disconcerting, almost human, expression (a very important feature). The Brussels Griffon is alert and lively, intelligent and full of confidence.

Bulldog

NON-SPORTING GROUP: USA/UTILITY GROUP: UK

Origin: The Bulldog has its origins firmly in Britain and his image has come to be synonymous with the perceived British persona of tenacity and stubborn determination — the legendary John Bull. The breed and its ancestors have been mentioned in works of literature throughout the centuries and is referred to by its old name, Bandogge, in Shakespeare's *King Henry VI.*

The Bulldog has been kept for a number of reasons over the years, as a butcher's dog to control unruly oxen, as a guard, as a hunter, but most commonly for the dubious practice of bullbaiting. Although the "sport" of baiting is now regarded as cruel and inhumane, the characteristics of the Bulldog, so loved by his devotees, came about as a result of breeders trying to produce the perfect dog for the purpose. A short muzzle and undershot jaw were necessary to ensure a vice-like grip, and the nose, placed well back into the dog's head, enabled it to breathe freely while gripping the fleshy nose of a bull.

Size & Substance: Weight UK: dogs 55lb; bitches 50lb. Weight USA: dogs 50lb; bitches 40lb.

Colors: The Bulldog can be white, red, fawn fallow, brindle, or red (with black mask or muzzle) with their various shades. White and pied (combination of white with any of the foregoing colors) are also permissible. The brindles, to be perfect, should have a fine, even, and equal distribution of the composite colors. In both brindles and solid colors a small white patch on the chest is not considered detrimental. In piebalds, the color patches should be well defined, of pure color, and symmetrically distributed.

Coat & Skin: The Bulldog's coat should be finely textured, straight, short, close, smooth, and glossy. The skin should be soft and loose, especially at the head, neck and shoulders. The head and face should be covered with heavy wrinkles, and at the throat, from jaw to chest, there should be two loose pendulous folds, forming the distinctive dewlap.

Temperament: Today, the breed is much loved for its affectionate disposition and ability to get along with other dogs and it is truly an ideal pet as its companionship with children is universally recognized. Alert, bold, loyal, and fearless, the Bulldog has a gentle nature despite its somewhat fierce appearance.

Bullmastiff

WORKING GROUP: USA & UK

Origin: This relative newcomer was only developed in the late 19th century by crossings of the Mastiff and the Bulldog. It was originally bred to assist gamekeepers on large estates in England in the apprehension of poachers. The dog was not meant to savage the trespasser but to restrain him until the gamekeeper arrived and originally a brindle color, which was difficult to spot at night, was preferred.

The breed was standardized by 1924, and recognized as the Bullmastiff in England then nine years later by the American Kennel Club.

Size & Substance: Height at shoulder: dogs 25-27in; bitches 24-26in. Weight: dogs 110-130lb; bitches 100-120lb.
The Bullmastiff is a muscular breed, with substantial bone development.

Colors: Any shade of brindle, fawn, or red with a black muzzle and black markings round the eyes.

Coat: The coat is weather resistant, short, hard, and lying close to the body.

Temperament: The Bullmastiff is an alert dog, courageous and faithful with high spirits — it makes an excellent companion.

Bull Terrier

TERRIER GROUP: USA & UK

Origin: In early half of the 19th century, the Bulldog and the now extinct White English Terrier were interbred to produce the "Bull and Terrier" later known as the Bull Terrier. The cross produced a lighter, more agile dog used to kill vermin and work in the pit.

Size & Substance: There are no height or weight limits but the dog must be strongly built, muscular, and symmetrical.

Colors: Pure white, brindle, black, red, fawn, or tricolor are all common. Markings on the head are permissible in the pure white.

Coat: This sould be flat, even, and harsh with a fine gloss and a soft textured undercoat in the winter. The dog's skin should fit tightly.

Temperament: Although sometimes obstinate the Bull Terrier is amenable to discipline. Its even temperament makes it very good with people.

Miniature Bull Terrier

Size & Substance: Height: should not exceed 14in.
This breed must be strongly built, muscular, and symmetrical.

Colors: As Bull Terrier.

Coat: As Bull Terrier.

Temperament: This is very similar to the Bull Terrier's although the miniature's diminutive stature, sense of humor, and natural ebullience can make him appear comical and clownish. Today's Bull Terriers are playful, fun-loving, and affectionate dogs who make wonderful pets and companions, despite their tough appearance. They are happiest when they are with the people they love and are miserable and unhappy if kept outside, away from human companionship. Although they will take as much exercise as is offered, they are quite content to spend time at home in warm and comfortable surroundings.

Cairn Terrier

TERRIER GROUP: USA & UK

Origin: Rough coated terriers resembling today's Cairn Terriers were recorded as far back as the 15th century, and by the late 1700s there was a large population of small terriers. These "Short Haired" or Little Skye Terriers, as they were known, were the likely result of crosses between the old White Terrier and the old Black and Tan Terrier and are thought to be the founding breed of all terriers. It was not, however, until the early 1900s that the formal name "Cairn Terrier" was designated to their descendants after the region in Scotland where they hunted fox, otter, and badger. The white dogs of this breed were also the forefathers of the West Highland Terrier.

Today, this long-lived, wonderful family dog is one of the most popular pets in the UK and in North America.

Size & Substance: Height at withers: 11-12in. Maximum weight: dogs 14lb; bitches 13lb.
The Cairn must be of balanced proportions.

Colors: Cream, wheaten, red, gray, or brindling in all these colors are all acceptable but whole white is unsatisfactory. Dark ears, muzzle, and tail tip are also desirable. It is worth noting that the color of the dog may change drastically while it is growing up.

Coat: The Cairn Terrier has a weather resistant, profuse, and harsh double-coat. The undercoat is short, soft and close.

Temperament: Fearless and assertive, but not aggressive, the Cairn Terrier's sporting ancestry always makes it always "ready to go."

Canaan Dog

HERDING GROUP: USA/UTILITY GROUP: UK

Origin: This natural breed of Israel dates back to pre-biblical times in the "Land of Canaan" where they first originated. Illustrations on tombs dating 2200-2000 BC depict dogs which show a remarkable similarity to the Canaan Dog of today. However, the Canaan population amongst the ancient Israelites was decimated when the Romans dispersed the Hebrew people over 2,000 years ago. The dogs sought refuge in the Negev Desert, remaining mostly undomesticated, although some retained a degree of domesticity, living with the Bedouin and guarding their herds and camps. Later, in the 1930s, the Canaan was developed to guard the isolated Israeli settlements and, as a breed, proved highly intelligent and easily trainable. During World War II, the breed served as sentry dogs, messengers, Red Cross helpers, and, as land mine detectors, they proved superior to the mechanical locators.

Size & Substance: Height: 20-24in. Weight: 40-45lb.
The dogs are larger than bitches.

Colors: Sandy to red brown desert colors are allowable, as are white and black.

Coat: The Canaan has a double coat — the outercoat is straight, harsh, and of medium length, while the undercoat is soft and short; density varies with the season.

Temperament: Sharp and alert, the Canaan is distrustful of strangers but devoted and docile with itsfamily.

Cavalier King Charles Spaniel

TOY GROUP: USA & UK

Origin: King Charles Spaniels of one type or another have existed in Britain since the 16th century, evolving from small dogs in a variety of sporting dogs' litters. The breed gets its name from King Charles II who personally kept a number of the toy dogs. The little dog was always popular with the British aristocracy and from the early 19th century the Marlborough family at Blenheim Palace bred a strain of small red and white spaniels. In the late 1920s, attempts were made to breed these little dogs to look like the ones depicted in the paintings of the old masters and, in 1945, the British Kennel Club granted the Cavaliers a separate registration.

The Cavalier King Charles Spaniel is the number one toy dog in England today and the purpose of this breed has always been that of a companion dog. It is the elegant royal appearance and typical gay temperament, along with the sweet and gentle expression generated by its large, round, dark brown, and warm eyes, which are of paramount importance in the breed.

Size & Substance: Height at withers: 12-13in. Weight:12-18lb.
The weight of the dog should be proportionate to its height and bone moderate in proportion to its size.

Colors: There are three common color variants: black and tan dogs should show a rich glossy black, with mahogany-tan markings. Tricolors have a ground of pearly white with black patches and tan markings, though the Blenheim has a ground of pearly white with chestnut-red patches. The ruby is a solid color of rich chestnut-red.

Coat: The coat is long, silky, and free from curl, although a slight wave is permissible. Feathering on the ears, chest, legs, and tail should be long — the feathering on the feet is a feature of the breed.

Temperament: The Cavalier King Charles Spaniel is a friendly and non-aggressive breed, without nervousness — it makes the perfect lap dog.

Chihuahua

TOY GROUP: USA & UK

Origin: Fact and legend gives the Chihuahua a very colorful history. Some theories argue that the breed originated in China and that examples were brought to Mexico by passing Spanish traders, while others feel that the Aztecs developed it. Maybe today's Chihuahua came about as a result of crossbreeding between the two. The true story of the breed may never be known but archaeologists have discovered remains of this breed in human graves in Mexico and in parts of the United States.

The modern Chihuahua is quite different from his early ancestors and this graceful, alert, and swift little dog comes in two varieties — long and smooth coated. The breed was named for the Mexican state of Chihuahua and first gained publicity towards the end of the 19th century. Today, the Chihuahua's size makes it a perfect pet for people who live in small city apartments and the little dog is one of America's favorite toy dogs.

Size & Substance: Weight: 2-6lb
This breed matures at around five inches tall at the shoulder and is definitely the smallest of the purebred breeds.

Colors: Any color or mixture of colors is acceptable.

Coat: The smooth Chihuahua is soft and, as it name implies, smooth; its fur will be close and glossy with a ruff on the neck preferred, but more scanty on head and ears. The rough variety will have a long and soft, flat or slightly wavy, coat with fringed ears.

Temperament: The Chihuahua is intelligent with spirited terrier-like qualities without being snappy.

Chinese Crested

TOY GROUP: USA & UK

Origin: Chinese Cresteds are recorded in China as far back as the 13th century and found their way to Europe and America via the busy trade routes.

It is generally recognized that over the years some hairless dogs have turned up in the litters of coated dogs as a genetic mutation. This is the case with the Chinese Crested — the Hairless, with fur only on the head, tail, and feet, and the Powder Puff, completely covered with hair, are two distinct varieties of this breed but are born in the same litter. The AKC accepted the Chinese Crested for full registration in 1992 and in that year there were four times as many of them at the Westminster Kennel Club's show than there were German Shepherds.

Size & Substance: Height at withers: dogs 11-13in; bitches 9-12in. Maximum weight: 12lb.
This breed is fine-boned and slender, though not so refined as to appear breakable.

Colors: Any color or combination of colors is permissible.

Coat: The Hairless variety should have fine grained and smooth skin with soft and silky hair on the head (crest), the tail (plume), and the feet, from the toes to the front pasterns and rear hock joints (socks). In contrast the Powder Puff should be completely covered with a double soft and silky coat.

Temperament: Both varieties of the Chinese Crested are extremely affable.

Chinese Shar-Pei

NON-SPORTING GROUP: USA/UTILITY GROUP: UK

Origin: The Chinese Shar-Pei is an ancient and unique breed, thought to have been in existence since the Han Dynasty in China around 200 BC, and its name literally means, "sand-skin."

The Shar-Pei shares the characteristic blue-black tongue found only in two other breeds — the Chow Chow and the Thai Ridgeback — possibly suggesting common ancestry. The breed was facing extinction in the 1970s until a famous appeal appeared in *Dogs Magazine* (April 1973) begging dog lovers in the United States to help save the Chinese Shar-Pei which was listed in *The Guinness Book of Records* as the "rarest dog in the world." Although originally bred as a fighting dog, this regal animal has today been sufficiently domesticated as to be described as a "people dog," preferring the companionship of humans to that of other dogs.

Size & Substance: Height at withers: 18-20in. Weight: 45-60lb.

Colors: The Shar-Pei can be either solidly colored — black or red — or have light and dark shades of fawn and cream. A solid color dog may also have shading, primarily darker, down its back and on the ears. The shading must be variations of the same body color and may include darker hairs throughout the coat.

Coat: Short, harsh, and bristly, the breed's coat stands straight off the main body and has no undercoat.

Temperament: The Shar-Pei is a calm breed and, although independent, very affectionate towards its own family. However, they can be somewhat standoffish with strangers.

Chow Chow

NON-SPORTING GROUP: USA/UTILITY GROUP: UK

Origin: This popular, massive Asian Spitz is one of the oldest recognizable types of dog — dating back more than 2,000 years — and it is commonly known that the Chow Chow owes its name to a Cantonese word for food (this is not to suggest that it was bred for this purpose).

The robust dog, with its distinctive blue-black tongue, was used for hunting, herding, and protection of the home in China. The Chow Chow arrived in the UK in the late 18th century and has remained true to type.

Today, its ancient lineage remains one of the main attractions to lovers of the breed.

Size & Substance: Height at shoulder: dogs 19-22in; bitches 18-20in. Weight: up to 55lb.
In every case, consideration of overall proportions and type should take precedence over size, although the breed should ideally be of medium size with strong muscular development and heavy bone.

Colors: The Chow Chow should be whole colored — black, red, blue, fawn, cream, or white — with lighter shadings in the ruff, tail, and abundant featherings.

Coat: Again, there are two varieties of this breed. The rough should have a rather coarse textured outercoat that is profuse, abundant, dense, and straight, and which stands off the body as well as a soft, wooly undercoat. The coat forms a profuse ruff around the head and neck, framing the head. The smooth variety has a short, abundant, dense, straight, and upstanding coat.

Temperament: Keen intelligence, loyalty, and independence, mark this breed. The typical "scowl" of this dog has in the past been misconstrued as a sign of aggression but it is simply the result of its deep set eyes and broad muzzle. The aloof, stubborn and somewhat suspicious nature of the Chow makes it difficult to train but once its affection is gained it makes the most devoted and delightful companion.

Collies

HERDING GROUP: USA/WORKING GROUP: UK

Rough Collie
Origin: All Collies originated in Scotland and it is accepted that they share some common ancestry though it has been argued that to make the Rough Collie more distinctive, certain crosses, including the Borzoi, were used. These Collies were utilized as working sheepdogs until the 1860s when Queen Victoria encountered the breed for the first time on a trip to Balmoral. She took some breeding specimens back to Windsor Castle and almost overnight the Rough Collie became highly fashionable. Later on, the *Lassie* films enhanced the breed's status as a loyal family companion.

Size & Substance: UK Height at shoulder: dogs 22-24in; bitches 20-22in. USA Height at shoulder: dogs 24-26in; bitches 22-24in.

Colors: There are four accepted color variations for this breed as follows. All should carry typical white collie markings:

ROUGH COLLIE

Sable and White — any shade of light gold to rich mahogany.
Tricolor — predominantly black with rich tan markings.
Blue Merle — predominantly clear, silvery-blue, splashed and marbled with black.
White — predominantly white, preferably with sable, tricolor, or blue merle markings.

Coat: This should be consist of a dense, straight, and harsh outercoat, with a soft and furry, very close undercoat. The coat is very abundant on the mane and frill while the face or mask is smooth.

Temperament: The Rough Collie is extremely affable, with no trace of nervousness or aggressiveness. A gregarious, loyal animal, it enjoys the company of people and makes an ideal family pet.

Smooth Collie
Origin: It is assumed that the Smooth Collie and the Rough Collie are different varieties of the same breed, but it is likely that the Smooth began life as a drover's dog and, in fact, the forefathers of the two varieties have less in common than is generally supposed. Later, with the advent of dog shows, there was much crossbreeding between the varieties until today, apart from their coats, there is very little difference.

Size & Substance: Height at shoulder: dogs 22-24in; bitches 20-22in. Weight: dogs 45-65lb; bitches 40-55lb.

Colors: As Rough Collie.

Coat: This should be a very dense, straight and harsh outercoat, with a soft, furry, and very close undercoat.

Temperament: As Rough Collie.

Coonhound (Black & Tan)

HOUND GROUP: USA

Origin: The origins of this breed can be traced back to an extinct hound from the 11th century and it also has elements of Bloodhound in its heritage as well as later traces of American and English Foxhound. The Black and Tan Coonhound is first and fundamentally a working dog, which can be used to track and tree raccoons, although it is powerful and agile enough, and has more than sufficient courage and stamina, to hunt deer, bear, and mountain lion. Much credit for the development of the modern hound must be given to the people of the US who live in the mountains of Virginia, the Ozarks, and the Great Smoky Mountains.

Size & Substance: Height: dogs 25-27in; bitches 23-25in.
This breed should show moderate bone and good muscle tone.

Colors: The accepted coloration is coal black, with rich tan markings above the eyes, on the sides of muzzle, chest, legs, and breeching, with black pencil markings on the toes.

Coat: The coat is short but dense to withstand rough going.

Temperament: This breed has an even temperament, and is outgoing and friendly. As a working scent hound, it must be able to work in close contact with other hounds. It is capable of withstanding the rigors of winter, the heat of summer, and the difficult terrain over which it is called upon to work and where it runs game entirely by scent. Due to the Black and Tan Coonhound's hunting instincts, it should never be turned loose or exercised unless within the confines of a securely fenced yard.

Dachshunds

HOUND GROUP: USA & UK

Origin: The Dachshund, low to ground, long in body, and short of leg was developed in Germany more than 300 years ago to hunt badgers — the German word "dachs" means badger. The breed's hunting spirit, good nose, loud tongue, and distinctive build make it well suited for below groundwork and for beating the bush, and its keen nose gives it an advantage over most other breeds for trailing.

The development of the hound differed in its native Germany to the UK where breeders developed a more exaggerated dog in terms of length and girth. In Germany, the less exaggerated "Teckel," as the breed is known, is still shown as a working dog. In the USA, the Dachshund owes its development to bloodlines from both countries and here the Dachshund is split into three varieties divided by coat not size — smooth, wirehaired, and longhaired. The development of the breed also produced the miniature and dwarf (Kaninchen) types.

Size & Substance: In the UK size is dictated by weight and the recommended standard weight is 20-26lb. Miniatures should be a maximum of 11lb.

Colors: All colors are allowed, though certain patterns and basic colors predominate. Single color Dachshunds include red (with or without a shading of interspersed dark hairs or sable) and cream: the nose and nails are black. Two-colored Dachshunds include black, chocolate, blue, and fawn — each with tan markings.

Coat: See below.

MINIATURE LONG-HAIR

Temperament: Good tempered, versatile, faithful, lively, and courageous sometimes to the point of rashness, the Dachshund makes a good companion whether you live in a small city apartment or the country. It must be remembered however, that despite their appearances Dachshunds are not sedentary creatures and they need plenty of physical exercise to maintain well being.

Standard and Miniature Smoothhaired Coat: This variety has a dense, short, smooth and shining coat.

Standard and Miniature Longhaired Coat: This is soft and either straight or slightly waved but always sleek and glistening.

Standard & Miniature Wirehaired Coat: Uniform, short, straight, and harsh with a dense undercoat. The distinctive facial furnishings include a beard and eyebrows.

LONG-HAIR STANDARD

MINIATURE WIRE-HAIR

Dalmatian

NON-SPORTING GROUP: USA/UTILITY GROUP: UK

Origin: The Dalmatian takes its name from a region in west Yugoslavia known as Dalmatia, but its origins aren't entirely clear as it is suggested that the breed has its basic roots in the English Pointer. Although the breed is mostly known as a coach dog, its role has varied over time from a dog of war, to a bird dog, shepherd, and retriever. During the Regency period in Great Britain the Dalmatian was a very popular "carriage dog" and it would run beside or under all types of carriages from those of the gentry to the mail coaches. In the USA, Dalmatians are also known as "Firehouse dogs" because they used to keep the horses under control before the advent of the fire engine.

Size & Substance: UK Height at withers: dogs 23-24in; bitches 22-23in. US Height at withers: 19-23in. The Dalmation should be strong and sturdy in bone, but never coarse.

Colors: The ground color is pure white with black or liver spots. In black-spotted dogs the spots are dense black, while in liver-spotted dogs the spots are liver brown. Spots are round and should be well-defined, the more distinct the better. The puppies are born solid white in color and only develop their distinctive spots later in life.

Coat: The Dalmation's coat is short, hard, dense, sleek, and glossy in appearance — neither wooly nor silky.

Temperament: Outgoing and friendly without a trace of nervousness or aggression, the Dalmatian may, however, appear snobbish with strangers, but it loves its family and has a great sense of humor — many of them actually smile when they are happy.

Dandie Dinmont Terrier

TERRIER GROUP: USA & UK

Origin: The Dandie Dinmont Terrier was originally bred to go to ground and is one of the oldest British terriers, originating in Northumberland during the 18th century. Its ancestry may lie with the old Otterhound but, in those days, the breed was known by its farm name or was called the Pepper or Mustard Terrier. The name Dandie Dinmont came from a character in Walter Scott's novel *Guy Mannering* (1814) who bred Mustard and Pepper Terriers — this is the only breed which takes its name from a literary source.

Size & Substance: Weight for a dog in good working condition: 18-24lb. Height at the top of the shoulders: 8-11in.
This breed is sturdily built with ample bone and well developed muscle, but without coarseness. The overall balance is more important than any single specification.

Colors: There are two accepted colorations for the Dandie Dinmont. Pepper ranges from dark bluish black to light silvery gray with a profuse silvery-white "top-knot." The hair on the legs and feet should be tan, varying according to the body color from a rich tan to a very pale fawn. Mustard ranges from reddish brown to pale fawn with a profuse creamy white "top-knot." The hair on the legs and feet should be a darker shade than the "top-knot."

In both colors some white hair on the chest is common.

Coat: This breed has a double coat — a soft, shiny undercoat, and a harder topcoat, crisp but not wiry. The head is covered with very soft hair, the silkier the better.

Temperament: The Dandie Dinmont is highly intelligent, independent, and determined, but also sensitive, dignified and affectionate as well as being tenacious and bold. It is fond of children, and makes a wonderful dog to live with. It is an excellent guard but is very strong willed and if it ever encounters a mouse or a rat its hunting instincts come alive. Always keep your Dandie Dinmont Terrier on a leash or in a fenced-in, dog-safe area.

Doberman Pinscher

WORKING GROUP: USA & UK

Origin: This breed was developed by and named after Louis Dobermann in Germany in the 1890s while he was searching for the ideal guard dog and companion. There is some argument, but most authorities think that a shepherd dog, the Rottweiler, a smooth-haired Pinscher, and a Black and Tan Terrier were the significant components of the breed.

The Doberman Pinscher is elegant in appearance, and of proud carriage, reflecting great nobility and temperament.

Size & Substance: Height at withers: dogs 27.5in; bitches 25.5in.

Colors: Black, brown, blue, and fawn are the accepted colors and rust red markings may occur with any of these.

Coat: This should be short, hard, thick, smooth, and close lying.

Temperament: Bold and alert, energetic, watchful, determined, and loyal, the Doberman is intelligent, fleet-footed, and fearless, but is very cautious with strangers and often unwilling to accept a new owner. Training this animal requires a firm but sensitive approach and it needs plenty of exercise and should never be allowed to roam loose. It is only when the Doberman is improperly handled that it may become aggressive and even bite. The well-bred and raised modern Doberman is a much more family orientated dog than the original bred by Herr Dobermann.

English Toy Spaniel

TOY GROUP: USA & UK

Origin: The Toy Spaniel made its first appearance in 17th century England during the reign of King Charles II. Due to the King's overt patronage of the breed it became very popular with members of the aristocracy who would have their portraits painted with their dogs, by the likes of Gainsborough, Rubens, and Rembrandt.

In the USA, the breed has appeared in the AKC's records since the club was founded, but in 1904, the AKC ruled that they should be combined into one breed, the English Toy Spaniel, and shown in two color varieties — King Charles and Ruby, and Prince Charles and Blenheim. The important characteristics of the breed are exemplified by the high and well domed head, which is large in comparison to size with a plush, chubby look, and large very dark brown or black eyes set squarely on line with the nose.

Size & Substance: Weight: 8-14lb
General symmetry and substance are more important than the actual weight. This breed should be sturdy of frame and solidly constructed.

Colors: There are four color variations of this breed:

Black and Tan: Glossy black with mahogany-tan markings.
Tricolor: The ground is pearly white with black patches and tan markings.
Blenheim: A ground of pearly white with chestnut-red patches. This often carries a thumb mark or "Blenheim Spot" placed on the top and the center of the skull.
Ruby: Rich chestnut-red.

Coat: The coat of the English Toy Spaniel is long, silky, and straight — sometimes with a slight wave — with heavy fringing on the ears, body, and on the chest. There is also flowing feathering on both the front and hind legs, and feathering on the feet.

Temperament: Bright, gentle, and affectionate, though somewhat reserved, the English Toy Spaniel is a bright little lap dog which was bred for the fireside not the farmyard and is affectionate, loyal, and willing to please.

Finnish Spitz

NON-SPORTING GROUP: USA/HOUND GROUP: UK

Origin: This dog, one of the Spitz breeds native to Scandinavia, is the national dog of Finland and, in its native land, contests are held annually to select a "King Barker." The Finnish Spitz (or Finsk Spets) is one of Europe's most ancient breeds, the pointed muzzle, small erect ears, dense coat, and curled tail denoting its northern heritage.

Size & Substance: Height at withers: dogs 17-20in; bitches 15.5-18in. Weight: 31-35lb.
Substance and bone should be in proportion to the overall dog.

Colors: The Finnish Spitz may be either reddish-brown or red-gold. As the undercoat is of a paler color, the effect of this shading is a coat that appears to glow.

Coat: Short and close on the head and front of the legs, the coat should be longish and semi-erect on the body and back of the legs with a short, soft, and dense undercoat.

Temperament: The Finnish Spitz is alert, lively, friendly, and brave although cautious and independent. Hardy, persistent, and very independent, this is a dog that naturally hunts game and is even bold enough to hunt bear but today, except in Finland where it is prized for its handsome fox-like appearance, it is primarily a house dog.

Foxhound (English)

HOUND GROUP: USA & UK

Origin: This heavy, round boned dog was bred in England to follow stag as well as fox. These dogs, with their distinctive "voice" when in pursuit of their quarry, were designed and reared by horsemen to be followed on horseback. Initially bred as workers, not much attention was paid to the color, size, or coat pattern of the hounds but, as time passed, the aim was focused to make a pack of hounds uniform in all respects and thus easily recognizable.

Size & Substance: This is unimportant as overall proportion and health are the main issue with this breed. However, a good specimen will have great bone and substance.

Colors: Any hound colors are permissable and tan marked with black saddle and white trim is the most popular, though lemon or red with white trim is found just as frequently.

Coat: The English Foxhound has a shiny, hard, typical hound coat.

Temperament: Any dog chosen as a companion must be well socialized and made to feel that its human family is part of its pack. Generally though, the Foxhound should not be relegated to the role of family pet but should be kept in a pack as a working animal.

Fox Terriers

TERRIER GROUP: USA & UK

Smooth Fox Terrier & Wire Fox Terrier
In the USA the Smooth and the Wire are considered as two separate breeds.

Origins: These terriers were originally bred in England to go to ground in pursuit of small game and are characterized by a hardy constitution and cocksure personality. They have a keen nose, remarkable eyesight, and excellent staying power. The Fox Terrier Club was founded in England in 1876, and the two coats were given separate registers. Through selective breeding, the head of the wire has become somewhat exaggerated though the smooth remains pretty much the same as its forebears

Size & Substance: Height at withers: dogs not exceeding 15.5in; bitches, slightly less: weight: dogs 18lb; bitches slightly less.

Color: White, white with tan, black, or tan markings are all ususal though white should always predominate.

Coat: The smooth variety has a smooth, hard, dense, and abundant coat that is straight and flat. The wire's coat will be dense with a very wiry texture. The best coats appear to be broken, the hairs having a tendency to twist, and are of dense, wiry texture, like coconut matting.

Temperament: Both of these terriers are fearless yet friendly and forthcoming. Alert and quick of movement — always "on the tiptoe of expectation," they are easily housebroken but their innate sense to dig comes out unless taught otherwise and they must not be let loose among livestock or poultry.

WIRE FOX TERRIER

French Bulldog

NON-SPORTING GROUP: USA/UTILITY GROUP: UK

Origin: The French Bulldog, with its distinctive bat ears is, to some extent, a smaller version of the larger, more exaggerated English Bulldog. The preservation of the bat ear as a distinct feature has been aided by the persistent efforts of American fanciers. The "Frenchie" has been around for over 100 years and, although there is a certain amount of disagreement as to its origin, the French vehemently claim that the breed is theirs.

Size & Substance: Weight: dogs 28lb; bitches 24lb.
This breed is muscular and heavy boned.

Colors: Three color variations occur. Brindle is a mixture of black and colored hairs which may contain white, while in the pied dogs white predominates over brindle. The fawn may contain brindle hairs, but must have black eye rims and eyelashes.

Coat: This should have a fine, smooth, lustrous texture and be short and close. The skin is soft and loose, especially at the head and shoulders, forming wrinkles.

Temperament: Extremely affectionate, intelligent, well behaved, and adaptable, French Bulldogs make very comfortable companions. Generally active, alert, and playful, but not unduly boisterous they are happy in any loving environment and are bred primarily as pets though they do make good watch dogs.

German Shorthaired Pointer

SPORTING GROUP: USA/GUNDOG GROUP: UK

Origin: The German Shorthaired Pointer was known in its native Germany as early as the 17th century and is a versatile hunter — an all-purpose gun dog capable of high performance in field and water. In Germany, the German Wirehaired Pointer is the most popular hunting dog but in the USA and the UK the popularity of the Shorthaired is greater than its cousin. These are two distinct breeds, not the same breed with different coats.

Size & Substance: Height at withers: dogs 23-25in; bitches 21-23in. Weight: dogs 55-70lb; bitches 45-60lb.

Colors: Liver, black, liver and white spotted, liver and white spotted and ticked, liver and white ticked, black and white spotted, black and white spotted and ticked. It is worth mentioning that black is not allowed in the USA.

Coat: This should be short, flat, and coarse — the coat is somewhat longer on the underside of the tail and the back edges of the haunches. The hair is softer, thinner, and shorter on the ears and the head.

Temperament: Alert, gentle, affectionate, and very loyal with a keen enthusiasm for work, the Shorthaired is a hardy dog who makes a great companion in the field or the home but, as it needs plenty of exercise, it is better suited for families who live in the country.

German Wirehaired Pointer

SPORTING GROUP: USA/GUNDOG GROUP: UK

Origin: In Germany during the late 1870s, sportsmen were searching for an all-purpose gun dog that could find game, point, and then retrieve it. Most of the early Wirehaired Pointers represented a combination of Griffon, Stichelhaar, Pudelpointer (cross between a Poodle dog and an English Pointer bitch), and the German Shorthair. The Griffon and the Stichelhaar were composed of Pointer, Foxhound, Pudelpointer, and a Polish Water dog. With this composition of forebears it is easy to appreciate the different hunting skills incorporated in the Wirehaired Pointers of the last century or so. Today, in its native Germany, the Wirehaired Pointer is the most popular hunting dog.

Size & Substance: UK height at withers: dogs 23-25in; bitches 21-23in. USA height at withers: dogs 24-26in; bitches are smaller but not under 22in.

Colors: Liver, liver and white, and black and white are all permissible though the latter is not allowed in USA.

Coat: The functional wiry coat is the breed's most distinctive feature and it should lie close to the body. A thick, harsh, and weather-resistant outercoat lies over a dense undercoat that is more prevalent in winter.

Temperament: The German Wirehaired Pointer is alert, gentle, affectionate, and very loyal although it may be aloof with strangers.

German Shepherd Dog

HERDING GROUP: USA/WORKING GROUP: UK

Origin: The German Shepherd Dog, Alsation or the "Shepherd," as it is known to most people, was the third most popular dog in the American Kennel Club list for 1998 and is arguably the favorite breed worldwide. Dogs may be shorthaired, longhaired and, very rarely, wirehaired and probably invoke a fiercer pride in their owner than almost any other breed. For all the bad press that the breed has unfortunately attracted over the years, it is agreed by all dog enthusiasts that a genuine German Shepherd is possessed of a truly steady temperament and will courageously face any adversity. The dog's propensity for trainability ranks with any breed and it has become the most widely used animal by police forces and the military all over the globe. Apart from its usefulness to the forces of law and order this dog's temperament also finds it rated with the best as a guide dog for the blind.

Size & Substance: Height from withers (and just touching elbows): dogs 25in; bitches 23in.
There is no specified weight but the dog should not look heavy or cumbersome.

Colors: The Alsatian may be black, black saddle with tan, gold to light gray markings, or sable (black or gray with lighter or brown markings).

Coat: The German Shepherd has a straight, hard, and close-lying outercoat that should be as dense as possible with a thick undercoat.

Temperament: This breed is extremely courageous, loyal, and self-assured with a steady nerve. Never nervous or shy, it is generally understood that this energetic, alert, and most determined of dogs needs an equally determined owner. Eagerness to work is an inborn quality so a Shepherd needs a firm, consistent hand, and constant interests to keep its highly intelligent mind occupied for it is when the dog becomes bored that there is a tendency to become mischievous.

Great Dane

WORKING GROUP: USA & UK

Origin: The earliest written description of a dog resembling the breed may be found in Chinese literature dating back to 1121 BC and further evidence links them to the ancient Greeks and Romans. The Great Dane (or German Mastiff) was further developed in Germany to hunt wild boars and is the most remarkable of all the Mastiffs with its svelte elegance and long head. It is not difficult to appreciate why the aristocracy of the time prized these noble beasts and desired their presence lying in front of the blazing hearth in their castles.

The name of the breed (in the English language) is a translation of an old French designation, grand Danois, meaning "big Danish," which is a bit of a mystery as Denmark has no real claim to the origins of the breed.

Size & Substance: Minimum height of adult: dogs 30in; bitches 28in. Minimum weight of adult: dogs 120lb; bitches 100lb.

Colors: There are five accepted color variations of the Great Dane:

Brindle: The ground color may be from lightest buff to deepest orange, and the coat must have black stripes.
Fawn: Lightest buff to deepest orange.
Blue: Light gray to deep slate.
Black: Pure black.
Harlequin: Pure white ground with all black or all blue patches.

The light colored dogs may have a black mask.

Coat: The Great Dane has a short, smooth, and sleek coat which must not stand away from the body.

Temperament: Friendly, outgoing, and considerate, the Dane can make a great family dog, but will usually commandeer the most comfortable seat in the house and will not hesitate to stretch out in front of the fire, blocking the warmth from the rest of the family.

Great Pyrenees

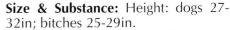

WORKING GROUP: USA & UK

Origin: Fossilized remains of this dog are found in deposits of the Bronze Age, which roughly dates its appearance in Europe between 1800 and 1000 BC, and makes it one of the oldest of the natural breeds. It is believed that it is descended from the Hungarian Kuvasz and came originally from Central Asia or Siberia, following the Aryan migration into Europe. The breed was developed further in the Pyrenees for rugged mountain work and the arduous task of guarding the flocks against wolves and bears in all kinds of weather on the steep mountain slopes.

Size & Substance: Height: dogs 27-32in; bitches 25-29in.
Weight should be in proportion to the overall size and structure of the dog. The Great Pyrenees is a dog of medium substance.

Colors: The Great Pyrenees should be either mainly white (with patches of badger, wolf-gray, or pale yellow) or solid white.

Coat: The breed has a coarse textured, thick and straight (or slightly wavy) overcoat and a profuse undercoat of very fine hairs. The coat is more abundant about the neck and shoulders where it forms a ruff or mane which is more pronounced in males.

Temperament: This breed exudes quiet confidence. It is strong willed, independent, and somewhat reserved, yet attentive, fearless, and loyal.

Greyhound

HOUND GROUP: USA & UK

Origin: The first recorded knowledge of the Greyhound dates back to between 2900 and 2751 BC and the Tomb of Amten, in the Valley of the Nile, where it was raised and owned by the ruling classes. The breed was traditionally used to hunt large prey such as deer, wolf, and wild boar, but in more recent years has been used for coursing and commercially profitable racing.

The Greyhound is the best-known racing dog and the fastest breed of dog — capable of speeds of nearly 45 miles per hour in short bursts. Despite the fact that they are trained to race at the highest possible speed, and breeders pay scant attention to factors such as coat, color etc., they are also one of the most popular show dogs in the USA. One of the most celebrated of many Greyhound owners in history was General George A. Custer who supposedly traveled with a hound pack that numbered about 40.

Size & Substance: Height: dogs 28-30in; bitches 27-28in. Weight: dogs 65-70lb; bitches 60-65lb.

Colors: The Greyhound may be black, white, red, fawn, blue, fallow, or brindle. Any of these colors can be broken with white.

Coat: Short, smooth, and firm.

Temperament: Gentle, affectionate, and intelligent, once retired from the track these dogs adapt easily to become all-round house dogs and good companions.

Harrier

HOUND GROUP: USA

Origin: Greek literature dating from around 400 BC has described small game, rabbit or hare, being hunted by a dog that very much resembles today's Harrier. Harriers may have traveled to England with the Normans whose word "harrier" meant hound. The first record of the breed in England was the Penistone pack established by Sir Elias de Midhope in 1260 to hunt hare. In the USA, they have been used for hunting since Colonial times.

Size & Substance: Height: dogs 19-20in; bitches slightly smaller. The Harrier is sturdily built and possesses large bone for its size.

Colors: Any hound color.

Coat: Hard, dense, and glossy.

Temperament: Harriers are friendly, gentle, and responsive. They are really a smaller version of the English Foxhound and are outgoing dogs which get along well with people and other dogs.

Ibizan Hound

HOUND GROUP: USA & UK

Origin: The similarities between this dog and the somewhat larger Pharaoh Hound have led to conjecture that it is descended from it. Ibizan Hound history is traceable back to approximately 3400 BC and Egyptologists have identified the breed depicted on artifacts discovered in the tombs of the Pharaohs. Later, in the eighth century, Phoenician sailors are said to have brought them to the island of Ibiza, and it is also thought that they accompanied Hannibal and his elephants on his arduous journey over the Alps.

Size & Substance: Height: 22-29in. Weight: dogs 50lb; bitches 45lb. This breed will ideally have clean, fine bones with the muscling being strong, yet flat, and no sign of heaviness.

Colors: White, chestnut, and lion or any combination of these colors is permissible.

Coat: The coat of the Ibizan Hound may be smooth or rough, but is always close, hard, and dense.

Temperament: This is an alert, affable, and intelligent breed, though Ibizan Hounds require a great deal of exercise and should only be allowed off the leash in a fenced in area. As these are very agile dogs, capable of jumping great heights from a standstill, it is recommended that the fences are at least six feet in height. Ibizan Hounds are very neat dogs who clean themselves much like cats.

Irish Terrier

TERRIER GROUP: USA & UK

Origin: The Irish Terrier is one of the oldest of the terrier breeds to come from Ireland, and also has the most personality. The first record of it being shown as a recognized breed dates back to 1875 in Glasgow.

Its fearlessness, coupled with its undoubted intelligence, made it very useful during World War I, when it was employed as a messenger dog in the trenches.

Size & Substance: Ideal height at shoulder: dogs 19in; bitches 18in. Most desirable weight in show condition: dogs 27lb; bitches 25 lb.

Colors: The Irish Terrier is either solid red, red and wheaten, or yellow and red.

Coat: This should be harsh and wiry, free of lock or curl, and with a finer, softer undercoat.

Temperament: Affable with human beings but with a tendency to be aggressive toward other dogs, this rugged, stout-hearted terrier is an absolutely loyal companion to its family and will guard them with utter contempt for its own personal safety. It is an affectionate, good-tempered dog, but is known for its "daredevil" attitude and for running headfirst, blind to the consequences of its actions.

Irish Wolfhound

HOUND GROUP: USA & UK

Origin: It is generally agreed that continental Celts took this breed to Ireland in around 1500 BC and, later, large Irish-bred hounds were given as gifts to the invading Romans. The first written record of the breed was in the year 391AD when the Roman Consul Quintus Aurelius received seven of them as a gift and "all Rome viewed with wonder." This is the tallest of all dogs and the modern name, Irish Wolfhound (Cu Faoil), has largely supplanted the previous appellations — "Irish dog," "Big Dog of Ireland," "Greyhound (or Grehound) of Ireland," "Wolfdog of Ireland," or "Great Hound of Ireland." In the mid-19th century, following the famine of 1845-46, the breed faced extinction until it was revived by a fastidious breeder by the name of Captain Graham.

Size & Substance: Minimum height: dogs 31in; bitches 28in. Minimum weight: dogs 120lb; bitches 90lb.

Colors: Gray, brindle, red, black, pure white, fawn, wheaten, and steel gray color are all acceped, with or without markings.

Coat: Harsh and rough.

Temperament: The Irish Wolfhound is friendly and gentle with a considerate nature. This rare breed requires great care especially during its first year of life and needs an owner who can give it time and companionship.

Italian Greyhound

TOY GROUP: USA & UK

Origin: The Italian Greyhound, although much smaller, is very similar to the more familiar Greyhound and is the smallest of the family of gaze-hounds (dogs that hunt by sight).

The breed is believed to have originated more than 2,000 years ago in the Mediterranean area, possibly in the countries now known as Greece and Turkey, and was one of the first breeds known to have been bred exclusively for companionship. It was a popular pet of Egyptian, Greek, and Roman aristocrats and much later was a favorite among many of the European royal families including Queen Victoria.

Size & Substance: Height: 13-15in. Weight: 6-10lb.

Colors: Black, blue, cream, fawn, red, and white are allowed, as is any of these colors broken with white or white dogs broken with one of these colors.

Coat: The Italian Greyhound has short, fine, and glossy hair, and its skin should be fine and supple.

Temperament: This is an intelligent and affectionate breed though it has a tendency to display aloofness.

Japanese Chin

TOY GROUP: USA & UK

Origin: Despite its name, this dog originated in China before it went to Japan. In the latter country, there are Inu and there are Chin and to the Japanese people the distinction needs no clarification. Chin are royalty, descendants of dogs that kept court with the ladies of the Imperial Palace and warmed the laps of the Chinese aristocracy. In the 1850s Queen Victoria was presented with a pair of these dogs by Admiral Perry on his return from his business expeditions to Japan and some 50 years later they found their way to the USA where they were known as the Japanese Spaniel until 1977.

Size & Substance: Height: 8-11in. Weight: 4-7 lb. The Chin is a solidly built breed, compact, yet refined.

Colors: Acceptible combinations of color are black and white or red and white. A clearly defined white muzzle and blaze are preferable to a solidly marked head.

Coat: The Japanese Chin has a profuse, long, soft, silky, and straight coat that is absolutely free from curl or wave.The tail is richly coated and forms a plume.

Temperament: The breed is extremely affable, gentle, and good natured. It is responsive and affectionate with those it knows and loves, but can be somewhat reserved with strangers.

Keeshond/Wolfspitz

NON-SPORTING GROUP: USA/UTILITY GROUP: UK

Origin: The Keeshond resembles the northern Spitzes with its profuse thick coat standing out from the body. In the 18th century the "armed Kees" was the mascot of the Dutch "Keeze" rebel party and the breed was named after the leader of the patriots — Kees de Gyselaer.

Today, known as the Dutch Barge Dog, it is popular in the Netherlands where it was originally used for hunting and guarding, although Great Britain was the country most responsible for the development of the breed.

Size & Substance: Height: dogs 18in; bitches 17in.

Colors: A mixture of gray and black.

Coat: Harsh, straight, and off-standing, with a soft, thick, and light-colored undercoat.

Temperament: The Keeshond is brave and friendly with an alert and marked guarding tendency.

Kerry Blue Terrier

TERRIER GROUP: USA & UK

Origin: As its name suggests, this dog originated in southwestern Ireland (where its name derives from the county of Kerry) and it was purebred in that area for over a century.

This all-round working and utility terrier was used in Ireland and England for hunting small game and birds, dispatching rats and other vermin, and for retrieving from land and water. In 1924, the Kerry Blue was officially recognized by the AKC and assigned to the Terrier Group.

Size & Substance: Height at shoulder: dogs 18-19in; bitches slightly less. Weight: dogs 33-37lb; bitches 35lb. The Kerry Blue should have a well-developed and muscular body.

Colors: Any shade of blue is usual, with or without black points.

Coat: Soft and silky, plentiful and wavy.

Temperament: This breed will display a charming disciplined friskiness.

Komondor

WORKING GROUP: USA & UK

Origin: This breed originated in Asia, where it descended from Tibetan dogs, but is now most prevalent in Hungary where it was brought over 1,000 years ago by nomadic Magyars and developed to protect flocks of sheep. It is one of the very specific groups of steppe cattle dogs that have a coat similar to that of a sheep. The working Komondor lives during the greater part of the year in the open and his coat serves to help it blend in with the flock and to protect it from extremes of weather and beasts of prey. It is a massive, strong dog and will only be happy when its difficult to maintain coat is kept clean.

Size & Substance: Height at withers: dogs 25in-31.5in; bitches 23.5in-27.5in. Weight: dogs110-135lb; bitches 80-110 lb.
Plenty of bone and substance.

Colors: Exclusively white.

Coat: The Komondor has a long, coarse, wavy, or curly outercoat with a softer undercoat. Hair clings like tassles, giving the coat a corded appearance like dreadlocks, the characteristic of the breed.

Temperament: This faithful breed is devoted but has a strong guarding nature which must be treated with respect.

A KOMONDER (right) with an Old English Sheepdog.

Kuvasz

WORKING GROUP: USA

Origin: This dog's name comes from the word "kawasz" which, in Turkish means "safekeeper," although it was in Hungary that the Kuvasz developed into the form in which it is seen today. This large dog's ancestors were giants in their country of origin, Tibet, and the breed is related to the Komondor, which had been brought from the Russian steppes by the Huns.

Size & Substance: Height at withers: dogs 28-30in; bitches 26-28in. Approximate weight: dogs 100-115lb; bitches a little less.
Bone should be in proportion to the body, which is of medium size, hard, and never heavy or coarse.

Colors: White only.

Coat: The Kuvasz has a double coat, which is medium coarse, wavy to straight. It is natural for the Kuvasz to lose most of the long coat during hot weather and a full, luxuriant coat grows in seasonally, depending on climate.

Temperament: A spirited dog of keen intelligence, determination, courage, and curiosity, the Kuvasz is happiest in a rural setting where it can have a large yard and can be kept outdoors throughout the year. This breed make excellent guard dogs and are careful with strangers, but sometimes aggressive with them. These animals are definitely not suitable for keeping as pets in city apartments.

Lakeland Terrier

TERRIER GROUP: USA & UK

Origin: This dog originated in the Lake District of Cumbria, England, where it was bred to hunt vermin in the mountainous setting and where its small, sturdy build is narrow enough to allow it to squeeze into rocky crevices.

The original Cumbrian terrier was known by several names according to its immediate locale; the "Black Fell," "Fell," "Westmoreland," and "Patterdale" amongst others. Eventually fanciers of the breed got together and by the beginning of the 1920s the name Lakeland Terrier was agreed upon.

Size & Substance: Maximum height at shoulder: dogs 14.5in; bitches up to an inch less. Average weight: dogs 17lb; bitches 15lb.
Balance and proportion are of primary importance and the dog should have sufficient bone and substance so as to appear sturdy and workmanlike.

Colors: Black and tan, blue and tan, red, wheaten, red grizzle, liver, blue, and black are the recognized colors.

Coat: The Lakeland Terrier has a harsh, dense, and weather-resistant coat with good undercoat.

Temperament: This is a courageous, self-confident, and friendly breed.

Lhasa Apso

NON-SPORTING GROUP: USA/UTILITY GROUP: UK

Origin: The Lhasa Apso originates from Tibet where it is known as "Bark Lion Sentinel Dog." There can be little doubt that this breed shares common ancestry with the Tibetan Spaniel and the Tibetan Terrier and has existed for many years. They were highly treasured by the privileged classes in their native country and few of them ever left Tibet. However, small numbers of Tibetan dogs did start arriving in Britain with military personnel at the beginning of the 20th century when they were known as "Lhasa Terriers."

Size & Substance: Ideal height at shoulder: dogs 10in; bitches slightly smaller.

Colors: The Lhasa Apso may be golden, sandy, honey, slate, smoke, black, white, brown, dark-grizzle, or particolor. All these colors are seen with or without dark tips to ears and beard.

Coat: This should be long, heavy, and straight with a hard overcoat (neither wooly nor silky) and a moderate undercoat.

Temperament: The Lhasa Apso is alert and unexcitable but somewhat aloof with strangers.

Maltese

TOY GROUP: USA & UK

Origin: This "ancient dogge of Malta" has been an aristocrat of the canine world for over 2,000 years and is generally accepted as being the most dramatic breed in the Toy Group. Since the time of Paul the Apostle there have been references to the Maltese and it is known that the Roman governor of Malta owned one.

The breed, like so many others popular in the US today, found its way to the New World via England where it was a favorite of Queen Elizabeth I.

Size & Substance: Maximum height at withers: 10in. Weight: under 7lb, with 4-6lb preferred. Overall quality is to be favored over size.

Colors: Pure white (slight lemon markings are permissible).

Coat: The Maltese has a straight and silky coat, never crimped or wooly. It hangs long over the sides of the body — almost to the ground.

Temperament: Affable, even tempered, and without fear, this breed is among the gentlest mannered of all little dogs yet it is lively and playful.

Manchester Terrier

TERRIER GROUP: USA & UK

Origin: The Manchester Terrier, "the gentlemen's terrier," was bred in the Manchester area of England to kill vermin and course small game and it is likely there is some Whippet in its ancestry.

Size & Substance: Ideal height at shoulders: dogs 16in; bitches 15in.

Colors: This breed should be jet black with rich mahogany tan. The tan should appear on the head and muzzle, which is tanned to the nose. The nose and nasal bone are jet black, but with a tan spot on each cheek and above each eye. The underjaw and throat are tanned with a distinct "V" and the dog's legs are also tanned from the knee downwards.

Coat: Smooth, short, and glossy — close and of firm texture.

Temperament: The Manchester Terrier is loyal, devoted but discerning, and keenly observant. Generally friendly with other dogs, as a sporting companion it is lively but not aggressive although, as a ratter, it can be relied upon to dispatch vermin quickly and efficiently.

Mastiff

WORKING GROUP: USA & UK

Origin: The Mastiff is from an ancient breed deriving from the famous Molossus hounds that were introduced into Europe by the Phoenicians. Since ancient times they have traditionally served as watch and guard dogs, mainly because they do not have the agility or stamina suited to other work. In English speaking countries the Mastiff is more properly described as the "Old English Mastiff" and in the past was used for the dubious deeds of dog fighting, bullbaiting, and bearbaiting. World War II took a great toll of the Mastiff population resulting in a reduction of the quality of the stock and this, allied with the difficulties in rearing the breed, means that the existing stock is not always of the best quality.

Size & Substance: Minimum height at shoulder: dogs 30in; bitches 27.5in. This is a massive, heavy boned breed, with a powerful muscle structure.

Colors: The Mastiff should be apricot fawn, silver fawn, or dark fawn-brindle, though the muzzle, ears, and nose must be dark in color; the blacker the better.

Coat: Short, thick, and close lying with a dense undercoat.

Temperament: The Mastiff is a courageous, steady, and affectionate breed but as a guard dog is wary of strangers. Dignity, rather than gaiety, is the Mastiff's correct demeanor.

Miniature Pinscher

TOY GROUP: USA & UK

Origin: The Miniature Pinscher originated in Germany and is older than its larger counterpart, the Doberman, although they are not in fact thought to be related. This breed, which is thought to be related to the German Pinscher, successfully made its way into the USA in the early 1900s and really began to establish its mark in Britain after World War II.

Size: Height at withers: 10-12in.

Colors: The Miniature Pinscher should have a black, blue, red, or chocolate coat with sharply defined tan markings on the cheeks, lips, lower jaw, throat, above the eyes, chest, lower half of forelegs, inside of hindlegs, and vent region.

Coat: This should be smooth, lustrous, hard, and short — closely adhering to and uniformly covering the body.

Temperament: This breed is alert and fearless for such a small dog.

Newfoundland

WORKING GROUP: USA & UK

Origin: Although there is uncertainty about the origin of this breed, most agree that the Tibetan Mastiff figured in its beginnings and that fishermen undoubtedly brought its ancestors to Newfoundland from the European continent. The dog has always been associated with Harold McPherson who governed the province of Newfoundland early in the 1900s and the artist Sir Edwin Landseer who depicted these dogs in many of his famous paintings. This gentle giant, with its webbed feet, water-resistant coat, and rudder-like tail, is a very powerful swimmer and, as a police dog, its duties have involved rescuing people from the sea. In 1919, a gold medal was awarded to a Newfoundland that pulled to safety a lifeboat containing 20 shipwrecked souls.

This is one of the most popular of the large working breeds and, apart from the breed's prowess in the water, it is still used in Newfoundland and Labrador as a true working dog, dragging carts and acting as a pack animal.

Size & Substance: Average height at shoulder: dogs 28in; bitches 26in. Weight: dogs 140-150lb; bitches 110-120lb.
The Newfoundland has considerable substance that is determined by spring of rib, strong muscle, and heavy bone.

Colors: Solid colors in the USA are black, brown, and gray, while in the UK, brown and black are accepted. The black is a dull jet black that may be tinged with bronze and the brown is chocolate or bronze. The "Landseer" dog is white with black markings only.

Coat: This is double, flat, and dense; of coarse texture with an oily, weather-resistant nature. The undercoat is soft and dense, although it is often less so during the summer months or in warmer climates.

Temperament: Extremely docile with a gentle disposition, sweetness of temperament is the hallmark of the Newfoundland and is the most important single characteristic of the breed.

Norfolk Terrier

TERRIER GROUP: USA & UK

Origin: The Norfolk Terrier's first recorded ancestors were a mixture of gypsies' dogs crossed with weavers' pets from Yorkshire and terriers from Ireland, and were very popular among sporting Cambridge undergraduates at the end of the 19th century.

Size & Substance: Ideal height at withers: 10in; bitches tend to be smaller than dogs. Weight: 11-12lb or that which is suitable for each individual dog's structure and balance.
Good substance and bone are essential in this breed and having the dog in fit working condition is a prime consideration.

Colors: All shades of red, wheaten, black and tan, and grizzle are recognized.

Coat: Hard, wiry, and straight, the Norfolk Terrier's coat lies close to the body with a definite undercoat.

Temperament: The Norfolk Terrier, originally the "drop-ear Norwich Terrier," is a "perfect demon" in the field where it can go to ground, bolt a fox, and tackle or dispatch other small vermin, working either alone or in a pack. This breed is fearless and alert, gregarious and loyal.

Norwegian Elkhound

HOUND GROUP: USA

Origin: The Norwegian Elkhound is a hunting dog that can trace its origins back to the Vikings era 6,000 years ago. In its native Norway it is still used to hunt elk, bear, and other wild animals. When the breed reached the USA the word "hund" was translated as "hound" rather than the current translation "dog," but the versatility of the breed as a hunter allowed it to remain classified in the Hound Group.

Size & Substance: Height at the withers: dogs 20.5in; bitches 19.5in. Approximate weight: dogs 55lb; bitches 48lb. The bone of this breed is substantial, without being coarse.

Colors: The Norwegian Elkhound is gray only with an undercoat that is clear light silver. The muzzle, ears, and tail tip are black.

Coat: Thick, hard, and weather resistant, this breed's coat is smooth lying with a soft, dense, woolly undercoat.

Temperament: The Norwegian Elkhound is bold, energetic, and loyal.

Norwich Terrier

TERRIER GROUP: USA & UK

Origin: In East Anglia, England, the fearless little Norwich Terrier was bred as a ratter to hunt vermin but today, in the USA, its status has been raised to hunt terrier. Arguments persist as to whether the "drop ear" (now known as the Norfolk Terrier) or the "prick ear" (Norwich Terrier) came first but, as many of the early Norwich Terriers had their ears cropped the truth may never be known. It is known, however, that the first "prick ear" champions bred in the USA came from "drop ear" parents. The two breeds were officially split by the British Kennel Club in 1964 and the AKC followed suit in 1979.

Size & Substance: Maximum ideal height at withers: 10in. Approximate weight: 12lb. This breed should show good bone and substance. Again, a fit working condition is a prime consideration.

Colors: Red, wheaten, black and tan, or grizzle are all permissable.

Coat: Almost weatherproof. Hard, wiry and straight, lying close to the body with a definite undercoat.

Temperament: Affable and fearless.

Old English Sheepdog

HERDING GROUP: USA/WORKING GROUP: UK

Origin: In early times this shepherd's or drover's dog was simply referred to as "the Shepherd's Dog" and today, because of its lack of tail, it sometimes goes by the fond name of "Bobtail." In 19th century Britain there was an excise duty on dogs that did not apply to working animals so, farmers used to dock the tails of their "Shepherd Dogs" to prove their lawful occupation and thus avoid the tax. The origins of the breed are unclear but it is almost certain that the Bearded Collie featured strongly in the original stock used to develop the breed. More certain is that the breed really began to develop in the hands of English West Country farmers looking for a good drover and guard dog. Along with the Bobtail's profuse coat, another distinctive characteristic of the breed is its resonant warning bark, loud with a deep ring to it.

Size & Substance: Minimum height: dogs 24in; bitches 22in.
The breed is well muscled with plenty of bone.

Colors: Gray, grizzle, and blue with a white head, neck, forequarters, and underbelly.

Coat: This should be profuse with a harsh texture, shaggy and free from curl.

Temperament: Courageous, faithful, and trustworthy, the Old English Sheepdog is always eager to please.

Otterhound

HOUND GROUP: USA & UK

Origin: Otterhunting was first mentioned in 1175 in England during the reign of Henry II though the early Otterhound probably included a French influence in its ancestry. It was originally developed to hunt otter because these creatures were depleting the fish stocks in the rivers and streams; but with the otter now on the endangered species list many of the once venerable packs of hounds have been disbanded.

Size & Substance: Approximate height at shoulder: dogs 27in; bitches 24in. Weight: dogs 115lb; bitches 80lb. The Otterhound shows good substance with strongly boned legs and broad muscles. It is a web-footed breed with membranes connecting the toes allowing the foot to spread.

Colors: Grizzle, sandy, red, wheaten, blue, black and tan, blue and tan, black and cream, liver, tan, and white — all the recognized hound colors.

Coat: This is long, rough, harsh, dense, and waterproof with a slightly oily texture and an undercoat which in the summer months may virtually disappear.

Temperament: The Otterhound is affable, easy going, boisterous, and has a melodious voice that it is known to use freely.

Papillon

TOY GROUP: USA & UK

Origin: The Papillon (meaning butterfly in French) is the modern development of those little dogs often seen pictured in rare old paintings and tapestries and was known in the 16th century as the dwarf spaniel. Marie Antoinette was an ardent admirer of the little dog, which is recognized by its characteristic butterfly-like ears.

An interesting drop eared variety of this breed is called the Phalene after the night moth of the same name which drops its wings.

Size & Substance: Height at withers: 8-11in. Weight: in proportion to height.
This breed has a fine-boned structure.

Colors: The Papillon should be white with patches of any color except liver. Tricolors — black and white with tan spots — are also acceptable.

Coat: Abundant, long, fine, and silky, the Papillon's coat falls flat on the back and sides. It has no undercoat.

Temperament: Alert, lively, intelligent, and friendly with no aggression.

Pekingese

TOY GROUP: USA & UK

Origin: The true origins of the breed lie hidden in the mysteries of ancient China but the wonderful legend of the Pekingese being the offspring of a lion and a marmoset can unfortunately be discounted. For centuries, there have been sacred dogs in China and the stone figures that decorate the ancient temples and palaces certainly bear a resemblance to the Pekingese but the ancestry of the breed can be traced back to the Tang Dynasty. Five specimens of the little dog were taken back to England in 1860 when soldiers of Britain and France marched on the Imperial Palace of Peking. The most illustrious of the five was presented to Queen Victoria and the breed's popularity took off in the Western world.

Size: Ideal maximum weight: dogs 11lb; bitches 12lb.

Colors: All colors and markings are acceptable, barring liver and albino.

Coat: The Pekingese has a coarse top coat with a thick undercoat. It should be long and straight, with a profuse mane extending beyond shoulders and forming a cape round neck.

Temperament: The Pekingese is loyal and fearless with a regal dignity tending towards aloofness. It can also display exasperating stubbornness.

Petit Basset Griffon Vendeen

Origin: The literal translation of the French dog's name sums up the breed: small (petit), low to the ground (basset), wire coated (griffon), and Vendeen — from the area in Western France the dog originated.

Size & Substance: Height at withers: 13.5-15in.
The dog should have strong bone with substance in proportion to the overall dog.

Colors: White with any combination of lemon, orange, tricolor, or grizzle markings.

Coat: This should be rough, long, and harsh to the touch. The Thick undercoat is never silky or wooly.

Temperament: A happy, extrovert, and bold dog with a good voice which he uses freely, the Petit Basset Griffon Vendeen is independent yet eager to please.

Pharaoh Hound

HOUND GROUP: USA & UK

Origin: The Pharaoh Hound is the national dog of Malta and Gozo and is thought to have been brought to the islands from Egypt by the Phoenicians over 2,000 years ago when they settled there. The paintings and the pottery discovered in the tombs of the Ancient Egyptians depict a dog which bears a remarkable resemblance to to the Pharaoh Hound of today.

It was from Malta that the first imports of the breed arrived in Britain, finally establishing itself in the 1970s. The first of the breed arrived in the USA in 1967, and the first American Pharaoh litter was whelped in 1970.

Size & Substance: Height: dogs 23-25in; bitches 21-24in.
This breed is best described as lithe.

Colors: The accepted coloration of the Pharaoh Hound is tan with white markings. A white tip to the tail is a highly desired trait as is a white mark on chest (called a star).

Coat: This can range from fine and close to slightly harsh and should be short and glossy.

Temperament: The Pharaoh Hound is alert, intelligent, affable, and high spirited. It is fast, with a marked keenness for hunting, both by sight and scent.

Pointer

SPORTING GROUP: USA/GUNDOG GROUP: UK

Origin: The Pointer, arguably the most distinct representative of the British gundog, originated in England around the middle of the 17th century. This breed is one of the world's best specialists at scenting and was the first dog used to stand game. It is generally accepted that the Pointers we know today were a result of crossbreeding a variety of Foxhound with the old Spanish Pointer. William Arkwright's volume on early Pointer history, finished around 1920, is still recognized as the basis of the breed.

Size & Substance: Height at withers: dogs 25-28in; bitches 23-26in. Weight: dogs 55-75lb; bitches: 45-65lb. Balance and overall symmetry are more important than size.

Colors: There are a number of recognized colorations for the pointer, including, lemon and white, orange and white, liver and white, and black and white. Single colors and tricolors are also both acceptable. In the darker colors, the nose should be black or brown while in the lighter shades it may be lighter or flesh-colored.

Coat: Evenly distributed, short, hard, and fine, the Pointer coat is perfectly smooth and straight with a decided sheen.

Temperament: The Pointer is an alert, considerate, and steady dog — dignified without timidity toward either man or dog. The breed's puppies appear to acquire their hunting instinct at an early age of around two months.

Pomeranian

TOY GROUP: USA & UK

Origin: The breed is undoubtedly a Spitz descended from the sled dogs of Iceland and Lapland but today's Pomeranian is of German origin. It has always been one of the most popular toy dogs and Queen Victoria was very devoted to the breed when it was introduced into the British Isles in the 19th century. In 1911, the American Pomeranian Club held its first specialty show and today Japan is considered to be the country where the best "Poms" are being bred.

Size & Substance: Weight: 4-6lb.
A good example of a Pomeranian should be medium-boned and sturdy; overall quality is to be favored over size.

Colors: White, black, brown (light or dark), blue (as pale as possible), orange (as bright as possible), beaver, and cream colors are all permissible as well as the following patterns.

Black and Tan — tan or rust sharply defined, (gray not permitted in UK).
Brindle — base color is gold, red, or orange-brindled with strong black cross stripes.
Parti-color — white with any other color distributed in patches.

Coat: A long, perfectly straight, glistening, harsh textured overcoat covers the whole body together with a soft and fluffy undercoat. It is very abundant round the neck and chest, forming a frill extending over the shoulders. The tail is profusely covered with long, harsh, spreading straight hair.

Temperament: The Pomeranian is a playful, outgoing, intelligent, and inquisitive breed.

Poodles

Origin: The Poodle is the national dog of France and it is not difficult to see why the fashion-conscious are attracted to them. There are many different styles, apart from the classic lion clip, in which this elegant and well balanced dog can be turned out, most of which derive from their duties as a retriever when balls of hair were used to protect their joints in cold water. The French gave the breed its name "Pudel" which roughly translated means "to splash in water." The dog is somewhat of a clown and at heart loves the attention drawn to it by the distinctive shapes and styles of his varied coiffeurs. Because of the breed's extrovert nature it was much utilized in the French circus and was, indeed, a very popular entertainer. This dandy is however very versatile and, as well as its history as a water and retrieving dog, it is very adept at searching out truffles for his gourmet owner. By 1960, the Poodle was the most popular breed of dog in the USA and remained so for the next 20 odd years and, although no longer "number one," it came fifth in a list of the most popular dogs in America, issued by the American Kennel Club in 1998.

(The words Standard, Miniature, and Toy are used to denote size only. All

MINIATURE POODLE FAMILY

three are varieties of one breed with the Standard Poodle being the oldest.)

Size & Substance: Bone and muscle of both forelegs and hind legs are in proportion to the size of dog.

Toy (USA Toy Group: UK Utility Group)
Maximum height at shoulder: under 11in; USA under 10in.

Minature: (USA Toy Group: UK Utility Group)
Maximum height at shoulder: under 15in.

Standard: (USA Group Non-sporting: UK Utility Group)
Minimum height at shoulder: Over 15 in, normally 21-26in.

Colors: All solid colors are acceptable. White and creams have a black nose, lips, eye rims, and toenails; browns have dark amber eyes, a dark liver nose, lips, eye rims, and toenails. Apricots have dark eyes with black points or amber eyes with liver points; while blacks, silvers, and blues have a black nose, lips, eye rims, and toenails.

Coat: In all sizes this is profuse and dense, harshly textured short hair that is close, thick, and curly. The traditional lion clip is recommended for show dogs.

Temperament: All Poodles are lively, affable, intelligent, and elegant.

TOY AND STANDARD POODLE

Pug

TOY GROUP: USA & UK

Origin: The Pug, one of the oldest breeds, has flourished true to its breed down through the ages from before 400 BC. It undoubtedly has its origins in the Orient but most breed historians agree that as the breed developed Holland was its home, before it arrived in Britain where its popularity soared. Many imports to the USA were the descendants of two specimens captured from the Emperor of China's palace during the Siege of Peking (1860) and brought back to England.

The initial wave of popularity for the breed quickly declined in the USA and by the turn of the 20th century their numbers had dwindled to zero. During the 1920s there was a revival and now, towards the millennium, the Pug is one of the top 30 dogs in America. This little animal has been referred to as "Multo in Parvo" translated as "a lot of dog in a small space."

Size & Substance: Weight: 14-18lb. Compactness of form, well knit proportions, and hardness of developed muscle characterize this breed.

Colors: Accepted colors for a Pug are silver, apricot, and fawn, with a black muzzle, ears, and markings on the cheeks, forehead, and trace that should be as black as possible.

Coat: The Pug's coat is smooth, soft, fine, short, and glossy, without being harsh or wooly.

Temperament: This Easy going breed has an affable and spirited disposition that is dignified and possessing great charm.

Puli/Hungarian Puli

HERDING GROUP: USA/WORKING GROUP: UK

Origin: The Puli has been an integral part of the lives of Hungarian shepherds for over 1,000 years, performing the arduous work of herding flocks of sheep on the open plains. Characteristic of the breed is the shaggy coat which, combined with its light-footed agility, has fitted it admirably for this centuries-old task. As with many breeds, its true origins have been lost with time but it bears a considerable resemblance to other Central European breeds and almost certainly shares common ancestry with the Poodle.

Size & Substance: Ideal USA height: dogs 19in; bitches 18in. Ideal UK height: dogs 17in; bitches 16in.
A medium boned breed.

Colors: This can be black, rusty black, white, gray, or apricot. The black dogs may have an intermingling of white hairs while the grays and apricots may have an intermingling of black or white hairs. The fully pigmented skin has a bluish or gray cast whatever the coat color.

Coat: The Puli has a dense, weather resistant coat — profuse on all parts of the body, it is wavy or curly, but never silky. It also has a soft wooly and dense undercoat. The correct proportion of top and undercoat creates naturally the desired corded effect.

Temperament: This spirited, affectionate, and intelligent breed is sensibly wary of strangers and therefore an excellent watchdog.

Retrievers

SPORTING GROUP: USA/GUNDOG GROUP: UK

Chesapeake Bay Retriever

Origin: The Chesapeake Bay Retriever evolved entirely in America and was descended from two shipwrecked Newfoundland puppies which were judiciously crossed with a variety of local retriever breeds, probably including the Curly Coat. The name is derived from the Chesapeake Bay in Maryland, which was their environs in their early sporting days.

The breed is known for it's prowess in swimming through rough, cold water, often having to break ice during the course of many strenuous retrieves of downed ducks and geese. However, it is equally proficient on land.

Size & Substance: Height at shoulder: dogs 23-26in; bitches 21-24in. Weight: dogs 65-80lb; bitches 55-70lb.

Colors: This breed can be brown, sedge, or deadgrass. Distinctive features include eyes that are very clear and of yellowish or amber hue.

Coat: The double coat consists of a short, harsh, wavy outercoat and a dense, fine, wooly undercoat containing an abundance of natural oil.

Temperament: The Chesapeake Bay Retriever has a bright and happy disposition, intelligence, quiet good sense, and an affectionate protective nature.

CURLY COAT RETRIEVER

Curly-Coated Retriever
Origin: This uniquely upstanding, multipurpose hunting retriever is recognized by most canine historians as one of the oldest of the retrieving breeds and is believed to have been descended from the 16th century English Water Spaniel and the St John's Newfoundland. The Curly was long a favorite of English gamekeepers, prized for its innate field ability, courage, and indomitable perseverance in retrieving small game and birds in the most appalling weather conditions and the iciest of waters. Its remarkable coat is completely waterproof and just requires a few shakes to be practically dry even after an arduous swim.

Size & Substance: Ideal height at withers: dogs 25-27in; bitches: 23-25in.
Bone and substance are neither spindly nor massive and should be in proportion with weight and height and balanced throughout.

Colors: Black or liver.

Coat: This breed has a dense mass of water-resistant, small, tight, distinct, and crisp curls. The coat is a hallmark of the breed and quite different from that of any other breed.

Temperament: This breed is self-confident, steadfast, and loyal as well as proud, wickedly smart, and highly trainable.

Flat-Coated Retriever
Origin: As a breed, the Flat-Coated was developed in the UK from stock that probably came from the Labrador and Newfoundland. It is very versatile, keen, and birdy — flushing within gun range — as well as being a determined, resourceful retriever on land and water. Towards the end of the 19th century the breed's popularity waned and by 1918 it was overtaken by the modern Labrador Retriever and then, at the end of the 1920s, by the Golden Retriever.

Size & Substance: Approximate height: 24in.
Traditionally described as showing "power without lumber and raciness without weediness."

Colors: Black or liver.

Coat: This retriever has a flat lying double coat of moderate length, density, and fullness, with a high lustre and moderate feathering on chest, back of legs, and tail.

Temperament: The determined and resourceful Flat-Coated Retriever is an affectionate, sensible, bright, and tractable dog.

Golden Retriever
Origin: The Golden Retriever is one of the most popular dogs in the world. In 1868, at his Scottish home Guisachan, Lord Tweedmouth famously mated a Tweed Water Spaniel to a yellow

FLAT COAT RETRIEVER

retriever and the resultant litter of four yellow puppies were the foundation of the definitive yellow breed now known as the Golden Retriever. The celebrated breed found its way to the USA with the help of Lord Tweedmouth's sons, one of whom lived in North Dakota and the other on the family's ranch in Texas.

As well as its innate field skills, this versatile dog has been a guide dog, a drug and explosives detector, and an effective tracker. The AKC recognized the breed in 1932 when the British Standard was adopted although this was later revised and is now much more detailed than the UK version.

Size & Substance: USA height: dogs 23-24in; bitches 21-22in. UK height: dogs 22-24in; bitches 20-22in.

Colors: A rich, lustrous gold of various shades is standard in the USA, while in the UK, any shade of gold or cream (excluding mahogany) is acceptable.

Coat: This should be flat or wavy with a water-resistant undercoat.

Temperament: The Golden Retriever is a stable, friendly, and confident breed.

Labrador Retriever

Origin: The Labrador Retriever is one of the best all-round dogs in the world. Its origins, however, are not from Labrador but from Newfoundland and lie with the St John's Newfoundland — later the "Lesser Newfoundland." This versatile relative of the Newfoundland is a powerful swimmer, even more accomplished than its Golden Retriever rival, and is one of the prime breeds selected as guide and rescue dogs. Like its celebrated Golden Retriever cousin, this breed has also been used by law enforcement agencies as a "sniffer" dog for drugs and explosives. Its sturdiness also enables it to work as a retrieving gun dog and to hunt waterfowl or upland game for long hours under difficult conditions.

Size & Substance: Height at withers: dogs 22.5-24.5in; bitches 21.5-23.5in. Approximate weight in working condition: dogs 65-80lb; bitches 55-70lb.

Substance and bone are proportionate to the overall dog.

Colors: Black, yellow, and chocolate are all permissable.

Coat: The coat is a distinctive feature of the Labrador Retriever and is short, straight, and very dense, giving a fairly hard feeling to the hand, though there is also a soft, weather-resistant, undercoat. A slight wave down the back is permissible.

Temperament: Intelligent, affable, outgoing, and compliant, the Labrador is eager to please and non-aggressive towards man or animal. A good temperament is as much a hallmark of the breed as the "otter" tail.

Nova Scotia Duck Tolling Retriever

Origin: The art of tolling involves a small dog frisking and leaping about in the water at the mouth of long funnel-like net with the purpose of luring ducks into the trap. This was practiced in Britain and Europe for centuries and, although no longer particularly popular in the USA, Little River, Nova Scotia, remains a bastion for these techniques. The Nova Scotia Duck Tolling Retriever has been developed from the Chesapeake Bay, Labrador, Flat-Coated, brown Cocker, and Irish Setter. This all-purpose dog is a good strong swimmer that changes from tolling to retrieving as soon as is necessary.

Size & Substance: Ideal height at withers: dogs 19-20in; bitches 18-19in. Weight: dogs 45-51lb; bitches 27-43lb.

Colors: This can be any shade of red or orange with some white markings.

Coat: The Nova Scotia Duck Tolling Retriever has a water repellant double coat of medium length.

Temperament: Like all retrievers, the Nova Scotia Duck Tolling Retriever is affable, playful, and compliant.

LABRADOR RETRIEVER

Rhodesian Ridgeback

HOUND GROUP: USA & UK

Origin: This dog was originally bred in its native Rhodesia to assist big game hunters in the pursuit of quarry which might have included lions. The characteristic feature of the breed is the ridge of hair that grows forward on his back, in the opposite direction to the rest of the coat. These days the Rhodesian Ridgeback is employed in its native Africa mainly as a guard dog.

Size & Substance: Height at withers: dogs 25-27in; bitches 24-26in. Desirable weight: dogs 85lb; bitches 70lb.

Colors: Light wheaten to red wheaten.

Coat: The Rhodesian Ridgeback has a short and dense coat that is sleek and glossy, but not wooly or silky.

Temperament: This breed is intelligent and dignified but aloof with strangers.

Rottweiler

WORKING GROUP: USA & UK

Origin: The origins of the Rottweiler are unclear but it is likely that the breed is descended from one of the drover dogs indigenous to ancient Rome as these are described by various accredited sources as having been of the Mastiff type. It does not take a lot of reasoning to understand why this marvelous beast was of such great value for cattle farmers through the ages and the Rottweiler's popularity was assured from Roman times all the way through to the 19th century. By the late 1800s, cattle driving was outlawed and, as the railway gradually replaced the dog cart, the Rottweiler's popularity declined. Today, this robust and well-muscled dog is utilized as a police dog in much of Europe where its intelligence and propensity for quick learning makes it ideally suited to the job.

Size & Substance: Height at shoulder: dogs 24-27in; bitches 22-25in. Approximate weight: dogs 100lb; bitches 115 lb.
The Rottweiler's bone and muscle mass must be sufficient to balance the frame, giving a compact and very powerful appearance.

Colors: This breed should be black with rich tan to mahogany markings, though a small white spot on the chest is acceptable.

Coat: The top coat is of medium length, coarse, and flat; the undercoat, which should be present on neck and thighs, must not show through.

Temperament: Despite having a reputation as a rather fierce dog, the Rottweiler should be calm, confident, affable, courageous, and biddable. Its natural guarding instincts make it a natural watchdog but it does require firm handling and thorough training.

Saint Bernard

WORKING GROUP: USA & UK

Origin: The massive Saint Bernard, "the famous savior of those who lost their way," is a much loved dog, popularly depicted by cartoonists with a trademark barrel of brandy around its neck. The most likely origin of the breed is that it developed from the breeding of the heavy Asian "Molosser" (*Canis molossus*), brought to Helvetia (Switzerland) by the invading Roman armies in first two centuries AD, with native dogs which undoubtedly existed in the region at the time. These dogs, referred to as Talhund (Valley Dog) or Bauernhund (Farm Dog), and widely used as guard, herding, and draft animals in the valley farms and Alpine dairies, were apparently well established by AD 1050. It was at this time that Archdeacon Bernard de Menthon founded the famous hospice in the Swiss Alps as a refuge for travelers crossing the treacherous passes between Switzerland and Italy. Folklore has it that the St Bernard could predict storms and avalanches and was used to sniff out travelers who had lost their way.

Size & Substance: USA Minimum height at the shoulder: dogs 27.5in; bitches 25.5in.
The British Standard says that the taller the dog the better, providing that symmetry is maintained. The breed's massive head is its trademark though female animals are of finer and more delicate build.

Colors: The St Bernard is made up of orange, mahogany-brindle, red-brindle, and white, with patches on body of any of these colors. Necessary markings for breed conformation include a white chest, feet, and tip of tail, as well as noseband, collar, or spot on the nape.

Coat: There are two varieties of St Bernard. The rough has a dense and flat coat, which should be full around the neck and plain to slightly wavy, though never rolled or curly. In contrast, the smooth has a close and hound-like coat, lying smooth without feeling rough to the touch.

Temperament: Very intelligent, even-tempered, courageous, and affable — given the proper training, a St Bernard will make an excellent watch dog though the owner will need a lot of space!

Saluki (Gazelle Hound)

HOUND GROUP: USA & UK

Origin: This "royal dog of Egypt" is arguably the oldest known breed of domesticated dog, identified by some historians as "a distinct breed" as far back as Alexander the Great's invasion of India in 329 BC. So esteemed was the Saluki in ancient Egypt that its body was often mummified like the bodies of the Pharaohs themselves. The Arabs were the first to breed the Saluki and, as they were a nomadic people, their much-prized breed was to be found over a vast area of the Middle East where sheiks have kept records of breeding and hunting abilities for centuries. The dog was initially bred as a courser and its great speed, strength, and endurance enabled it to kill gazelle or other quarry over the deep sands or rocky, mountainous terrain of its native lands. The American Kennel Club officially recognized the Saluki in 1927.

Size & Substance: Height at shoulder: dogs 23-28in; bitches proportionately smaller.

Colors: The Saluki is found in white, cream, fawn, golden-red, grizzle, silver grizzle, deer grizzle, tricolor (white, black, and tan), and black and tan, or any variations of these colors.

Coat: This should be smooth and silky in texture with feathering on the legs and back of the thighs between hock and heel.

Temperament: The Saluki is best described as a dignified breed and is intelligent and independent though somewhat aloof and reserved with strangers.

Samoyed

WORKING GROUP: USA & UK

Origin: This very ancient breed, originally kept as an all-purpose working dog, takes its name from the Samoyed people (now known as the Nenetsky people) of the Siberian tundra. These sledge dogs were crucial to the survival of the nomadic tribes who utilized them to herd reindeer and to warn them of approaching danger such as marauding wolves. The Samoyed was first introduced into northern Europe and Alaska, and from the latter into the rest of the USA, after the first Arctic expeditions.

Interest in the breed developed in the UK at the end of the 19th century after a Mr Kilburn Scott brought a puppy from the Samoyed homeland. The Princess de Montyglyon introduced the first of the breed to the USA in 1906, having been given it as a present by Grand Duke Nicholas of Russia. In the early 20th century this hardy sledge dog became very popular and today it is even kept as a pet in town apartments.

Size & Substance: USA height at withers: dogs 21-23in; bitches 19-21in. UK height at shoulder: dogs 20-22in; bitches 18-20in.
The dog's weight must be in good proportion to its size.

Colors: The Samoyed will be pure white, white and biscuit, or cream and its outercoat silver tipped.

Coat: The breed has a thick, close, soft, and short undercoat with harsh hair (not wiry) growing through it, forming a weather-resistant outercoat which stands away from the body and must be free of curl.

Temperament: Extremely affable to humans, The Samoyed is intelligent, gentle, loyal, adaptable, alert, full of action, and eager to serve.

Schipperke

NON-SPORTING GROUP: USA/UTILITY GROUP: UK

Origin: The Schipperke, its name believed to mean "little captain," is not a member of the Spitz or northern sled dog breeds although it resembles them in some regards. It is popular on the canals of Netherlands and in Belgium where it is utilized as a watchdog on the barges.

An agile, active hunter of vermin, the Schipperke originated in the Flemish provinces of Belgium and is descended from the Belgian Sheepdog or Leauvenaar. The Queen of Belgium bought a Schipperke in 1885, ensuring its popularity in Europe, and three years later the first of the breed was introduced into the USA although it was not until much later that it achieved popularity there.

Size & Substance: Suggested height at the highest point of the withers: dogs 11-13in; bitches 10-12in.
In this breed quality should always take precedence over size.

Colors: Usually black, however in the UK other whole colors are allowed.

Coat: The abundant and straight coat of the Schipperke is slightly harsh to the touch. A softer undercoat, dense and short on the body and very dense around the neck, makes the ruff stand out. The adult coat is highly characteristic and must include several lengths growing naturally in a specific pattern.

Temperament: Confident and curious, independent yet faithful, the Schipperke is reserved with strangers and stands ready to protect its family and property if necessary.

Schnauzer

The Schnauzer family is a group of three breeds and is the only one that takes its name from one of its own kind. Schnauzer, roughly translated as "small beard," was the name of a much-admired rough-coated dog that won its own class at the 1879 Hanover Dog Show.

Miniature
Terrier Group: USA/Utility Group: UK
Origin: It is believed that the Miniature was derived from a cross between the Standard Schnauzer and the Affenspinscher. Miniatures were first imported into the UK in 1928 from America where the breed had been introduced a few years earlier.

Size & Substance: Ideal height: dogs 14in; bitches 13in.

Colors: The Breed conformation allows all pepper and salt colors in even proportions, as well as pure black and black and silver (solid black with silver markings).

Coat: The Miniature Schnauzer has a harsh, short, and wiry coat with a dense undercoat and harsh hair on its legs.

Temperament: This breed is alert, reliable, and intelligent.

MINIATURE SCHNAUZER

Standard
Working Group: USA/Utility Group: UK
Origin: The Standard or Medium Schnauzer is the prototype of the three sizes that are bred and registered as distinct breeds. Its origins lie 15th and 16th century Germany where the breed was held in high regard as a household companion — its portrait appearing in many of the works of the Great Masters such as Rembrandt and the English painter Sir Joshua Reynolds.

The breed was originally classed as a terrier in America whereas, in its native land it was first exhibited as a Wire-Haired Pinscher — German breeders have always regarded the Schnauzer principally as a working dog whose tasks were that of rat catcher, yard dog, and guard. As the breed developed the dogs proved excellent catchers of vermin and were even capable of catching something for the pot if necessary. Prior to World War I, 90 percent of German farmer's dogs were of strong Schnauzer blood.

Size & Substance: Ideal height at withers: dogs 19in; bitches 18in.
This is a heavy-set dog with good muscle and plenty of bone.

Colors: The Standard can be either pure black, or pepper and salt ranging from dark iron gray to light gray.

Coat: As Miniature.

Temperament: As Miniature.

Giant
Working group: USA & UK
Origin: Originally bred in Germany for driving cattle and guarding, the Giant Schnauzer became one of the principal breeds for police and security work in Europe. Because of its size and working ability it was moved from the Utility Group to the Working Group in the UK during the 1970s.

Size & Substance: Height: dogs 25-28in; bitches 24-26in.

Colors: As Miniature and Standard.

Coat: As Miniature and Standard.

Temperament: The Giant Schnauzer is bold, affable, reliable, and composed.

STANDARD SCHNAUZER

GIANT SCHNAUZER

Scottish Deerhound

HOUND GROUP: USA & UK

Origin: Scottish Highland history and folklore going back nearly 1,000 years attests to the presence of mighty hounds that could chase and bring down Red Deer in the hills and glens. By the early 18th century the breed was perilously close to extinction, but thanks to the efforts of Archibald McNeill and his brother Lord Colonsay the best bloodlines available were used to start the Colonsay strain which persists into the 20th century.

Size & Substance: Minimum height at withers: dogs 30in; bitches 28in. Weight: dogs 85-110lb; bitches 75-95lb.

Colors: The Deerhound's accepted colors are dark blue-gray, darker and lighter grays, brindle, yellow and sandy-red, or red fawns with black points.

Coat: This is thick, close lying, ragged, harsh or crisp to the touch. Shaggy but not overcoated.

Temperament: Gentle and affable, docile, obedient, and compliant yet dignified, the Scottish Deerhound, with its keen hunting abilities is of greater speed and endurance than its near relation, the Irish Wolfhound, and, although more accustomed to the show ring today, one feels that its true place should be lying in front of a blazing log fire in the baronial hall of some great Highland castle.

Scottish Terrier

TERRIER GROUP: USA & UK

Origin: Due to selective breeding, the Scottish Terrier is one of the five different Scottish breeds of terriers that have developed. The Scottish Terrier type was originally favored in the Aberdeen area and for several years they were actually called Aberdeen Terriers, but it wasn't long before they found their way to England and America. The first show to have a class for the Scottish Terrier was in 1860 and the first registered Scottie in America was "Dake," whelped on September 15, 1884. This breed's wiry coat and thick-set, cobby body, erect ears, and tail, joined with his unique "varminty" expression, are salient features of the Scottie — nicknamed the "Diehard."

Size & Substance: Height at withers: 10-11in. Weight: dogs 19-23lb; bitches 18-21lb.
A thick body and heavy bone are essential to this breed.

Colors: Black, wheaten, or brindle of any shade.

Coat: The Scottie has a close-lying, double coat. The undercoat is short, dense, and soft; and the outercoat harsh, dense, and wiry — together making a weather-resistant covering.

Temperament: This is a bold, dependable, and loyal breed, but may sometimes appear aloof and independent. This is not a docile pet and can occasionally have a temper.

Sealyham Terrier

TERRIER GROUP: USA & UK

Origin: During the middle to late 19th century, many "go to ground" dogs were being developed to meet the perceived needs of sportsmen. Captain Edwardes bred the Sealyham Terrier at his estate at Sealyham, Pembrokeshire, in Wales, to hunt badger, rabbit, and fox. His aim was to produce a dog that would be bold and tenacious yet small enough to "go to ground" to prevent the prey from tunneling away before the sportsman could get to it. Most importantly, Edwardes who had seen the fate of small brown dogs emerging from a fox-hole into the jaws of a pack of hounds, determined that his new breed should be predominantly white.

There are no specific records but it seems that stock from the Welsh Corgi, the Fox Terrier, and the West Highland White were included in the breeding and development of the Sealyham.

Size & Substance: Maximum height at shoulder: 12in. Ideal weight: dogs 20lb; bitches 18lb.

Colors: The Sealyham should be all white, or white with lemon, brown, or blue. It may also have badger pied markings on the head and ears.

Coat: Long and hard, with a wiry top-coat and weather-resistant undercoat.

Temperament: Affable, alert, and fear-less, the Sealyham is a devoted and faithful companion.

Setters

SPORTING GROUP: USA/GUNDOG GROUP: UK

English Setter
Origin: The English Setter, one of the most glamorous of all breeds, was trained as a bird dog in England more than 400 years ago and has been mentioned in European literature since the 14th century. The first recorded breeder of English Setters was Edward Laverack whose pedigrees date to around 1860, and following the line was Purcell Llewellin who purchased from Laverack and introduced various outcrosses. The "Llewellin Setter" has a separate register in the USA with its own Field Stud Book, but it must be remembered that both types originated with the Laverack.

Size & Substance: USA height: dogs 25in; bitches 24in. UK height: dogs 25.5-27in; bitches 24-25.5in.

Colors: Several colors occur, which have special names — the Blue Belton is black and white, the Orange Belton is orange and white, the Lemon Belton, lemon and white, and the Liver Belton, liver and white. There are also tricolor dogs which are either Blue Belton and tan or Liver Belton and tan.

Coat: A good example of the English Setter will have a flat, long, and silky coat, which should be slightly wavy but not curly.

Temperament: The English Setter is a very affable and good natured breed.

ENGLISH SETTER

Gordon Setter
Origin: It was in the late 1700s that the fourth Duke of Gordon first started to stabilize this breed of black and tan setter in its native land of Scotland. His main interest was to breed the best working dogs for the field, but, when the Gordon Kennels were passed on to the sixth Duke, more attention was paid to standardizing the appearance

and type. In 1842, George Blunt and Daniel Webster introduced the breed to the USA and today, American breeders strive to keep the working ability of the Gordon strong and its appearance uniform.

Size & Substance: USA height at shoulder: dogs 24-27in; bitches 23-26in. Weight: dogs 55-80lb; bitches 45-70lb. UK height: dogs 26in; bitches 24.5in. Weight: dogs 65lb; bitches 56lb.
With plenty of bone and substance, this dog is the most powerful of all the Setters.

Colors: The English Setter may be deep, shining coal black without rustiness, or mahogany red with markings over the eyes, on the muzzle, throat, chest, feet, inside of the hind legs, and under the tail.

Coat: The beautiful coat is a characteristic of this breed and should be soft and shining, flat and straight or slightly waved, but not curly.

Temperament: The English Setter is bold, outgoing, steady, compliant, intelligent, and capable.

Irish Red and White Setter
Origin: This elegant and eye-catching dog is descended from the Land Spaniel from around the mid-17th century. The Irish Red and White Setter derives from the same root stock as the Irish Setter but, although it may even have been its predecessor, it should not be confused with its close relation. By the end of the 19th century the popularity of the solid red Irish Setter had all but eclipsed the Red and White and it nearly became extinct. However, it was successfully revived during the 1920s and today is a very popular breed across the whole of the British Isles. There is also a steady demand from overseas and several enthusiasts in the USA have received foundation stocks.

Size & Substance: Height: dogs 24-26in; bitches 2in less.

Colors: This is a clearly parti-colored breed; the base color is pearl white with solid red patches.

Coat: The Red and White has a finely textured coat with good feathering and a slight wave, but never curly.

Temperament: This breed is happy, affable, and affectionate.

Irish Setter

Origin: Setting Spaniels were used as early as the 14th century and were, undoubtedly, the ancestors of the Irish Setter. Its earliest progenitors were not solid red, but red and white with the solid red Irish Setter first appearing in Ireland in the 19th century. As early as 1812, the Earl of Enniskillan would only have self-colored dogs in his kennel. The color controversy continued through the 19th century until the 1870s, when the Irish Setter came to mean a solid red dog.

Size & Substance: Ideal height at withers: dogs 27ins; bitches 25in. Weight: dogs 70lb; bitches 60lb.
The Irish Setter is a sturdy dog, with plenty of bone.

Colors: This breed is invariably a rich chestnut with no trace of black at all. However, either a small amount of white on the chest, throat, or toes, or a narrow centered streak on the skull is acceptable.

Coat: The coat should be a moderate length, flat and as free as possible from curl or wave; short and fine on the head, front of legs, and tips of ears.

Temperament: The Irish Setter must rank amongst the most glamorous of all breeds. Openly affectionate, an outgoing, stable temperament is the essence of this dog. It is also a very accomplished bird dog with a good nose and the propensity to be an able retriever.

IRISH SETTER

Shetland Sheepdog

HERDING GROUP: USA/WORKING GROUP: UK

Origin: The Shetland Islands, lying to the northeast of the Scottish mainland, can lay claim to a number of small animals — notably the Shetland Pony and the Shetland Sheepdog. The "Sheltie" is a miniature Collie and this breed now bears the same relationship in size and general appearance to the Rough Collie as the Shetland Pony does to some of the larger breeds of horses.

It originated in the Shetland Islands as a small herding dog and, like the Collie, traces its ancestry to the Border Collie of Scotland. Its founders were transported to the Shetland Islands where they were crossed with the small, longhaired Hebridean breeds and reduced to miniature proportions. It is known as "a smaller species of one of the most beautiful of British breeds, the Collies of Scotland." The Shetland Sheepdog of the British Isles continues to be a smaller, lighter boned dog than its American off-spring.

Size: USA height at the shoulder: 13-16in. UK ideal height at withers: dogs 14.5in; bitches 14in.

Colors: A variety of colors are accepti-ble in this breed:

Sable: Any color from pale gold to deep mahogany — rich in tone, clear or shaded.
Tricolors: Intense black on the body, with rich tan markings preferred.
Blue Merle: Clear silvery blue splashed and marbled with black. Rich tan markings are, again, pre-ferred, although the general effect must be blue.
Black and White: White markings may appear in blaze, collar, chest, frill, legs, and on the tip of the dog's tail.
Black and Tan: This is also a recognized color variety.

Coat: The Shetland Sheepdog's outercoat is long, harsh textured, and straight, and its undercoat soft, short, and dense enough to give the entire coat its "standoff" quality. There should also be an abundant mane and frill, while the face is smooth.

Temperament: Affable and compliant with its owner, the Shetland Sheepdog is reserved towards strangers.

Shiba Inu

NON-SPORTING GROUP: USA/UTILITY GROUP: UK

Origin: This breed from Japan is still only registered in the "import register" in the UK. However, it is the oldest and smallest of Japan's dogs and was originally developed for hunting by sight and scent in the dense undergrowth of Japan's mountainous areas. With its ability to manoeuver steep hills and mountain slopes as well as its keen senses it was a superb hunting dog. Because of the World War II, and an outbreak of distemper in 1952, the Shiba Inu faced extinction and only three bloodlines remained at the time — the San In Shiba, Mino Shiba, and the Shin Shu Shiba. It is from these that the breed evolved into the modern Shiba Inu.

Size & Substance: Ideal height: dogs 15.5in; bitches 14.5in. Average weight at preferred size: dogs approximately 23lb; bitches approximately 17lb.

Colors: Red, black, black and tan, brindle, or white with a red or gray tinge.

Coat: A hard, straight outercoat covers the Shiba Inu's soft dense undercoat. Hair on the tail is slightly longer and stands open in a brush.

Temperament: The Shiba Inu is marked by a bright, active, keen, and alert personality. While it may be reserved toward strangers, it is loyal and affectionate to those who earn its respect.

Shih Tzu

TOY GROUP: USA/UTILITY GROUP: UK

Origin: The Shih Tzu's name means "lion" and this breed existed in the Far East as long ago as AD 624. There are many theories as to the exact origin of the Shih Tzu, all concerning Far Eastern nobility, but whatever the truth, it is known they were selected with great care for court breeding. The specimens most favored by the Emperors were portrayed in Chinese paintings and it is sometimes called the "chrysanthemum-faced dog" because of the way the hair grows about the face in all directions, resembling that bloom. The Shih Tzu was granted recognition by the AKC in 1969.

Size & Substance: USA ideal height at withers: 9-10.5in but not less than 8in, nor more than 11in. Ideal weight of mature dogs: 9-16lb. UK maximum height at withers: 10.5in. Weight: 10-18lb; ideally 10-16lb.
Regardless of size, the Shih Tzu is always compact, solid, and carries good weight and substance.

Colors: All colors are permissable and a white blaze on the forehead and a white tip to the tail are highly desirable in parti-colors.

Coat: This should be long and dense with a good undercoat, not curly but a slight wave is permitted. The hair on the head is usually tied up.

Temperament: The Shih Tzu is independent, but affable and affectionate.

Siberian Husky

WORKING GROUP: USA & UK

Origin: The people of the snowy northern climes have always utilized dogs to drag their loads or act as beasts of burden. Originating in Siberia about 3,000 years ago, the Chukchi people bred this animal as an endurance sled dog. Sledge dogs are still invaluable in these parts and, today, the dogs are not used solely for practical purposes but are also trained for sport. Dog races between individual dogs or teams are gaining in popularity all the time and the Siberian Husky, with its compact body build and smooth gait, is the fastest of the sledge dogs.

The breed was brought to Alaska in 1909, with the first team of Siberian Huskies making its appearance in the All Alaska Sweepstakes Race of that year. For the next decade, Siberian Huskies captured most of the racing titles in Alaska, where the rugged terrain was ideally suited to the endurance capabilities of the breed. Similarly, the Byrd Antarctic expeditions were made possible because of the use of this famous breed.

Size & Substance: Height at withers: dogs 21-23.5in; bitches 20-22in. Weight: dogs 45-60lb; bitches 35-50lb. This breed is of medium size, with moderate bone and well balanced proportions.

Colors: All colors from black to pure white are permitted. A variety of markings on the head is common, including many striking patterns not found in other breeds.

Coat: The Siberian Husky has a double coat that is medium in length, giving a well furred appearance. The undercoat is soft, dense, and sufficiently long to support the outercoat. A bushy tail and densely coated paws are also characteristic of this very attractive breed.

Temperament: A friendly and gentle dog, the Siberian Husky is outgoing and alert, intelligent and compliant.

Silky Terrier

TOY GROUP: USA & UK

Origin: Developed around the turn of the century in Australia from crossings of native Australian Terriers and imported Yorkshire Terriers, this breed was originally known as the Sydney Silky Terrier. However, in 1955, the official name for the breed became the Australian Silky Terrier. Most Australian breeds are primarily derived from the bush country but it seems likely that this one was bred solely as an urban pet, although it is a good ratter and is also adept at killing snakes which are numerous in its native land. The Silky Terrier with its glorious coat is a true "toy terrier."

Size & Substance: Approximate height at withers: dogs 9in; bitches slightly less. Most desirable weight: 8-10lb. This is a lightly built breed with strong but rather fine bone.

Colors: The Silky Terrier may be blue and tan or gray-blue and tan although there is a preference for richer colors. Coloration consists of a silver-blue or fawn "top-knot," and tan around the base of ears, muzzle, and the side of cheeks. The dog should be blue from the base of skull to the tip of the tail, also running down the forelegs and thighs, while a tan line should be showing down the stifles and from the knees and hocks to the toes.

Coat: Straight, fine, glossy, and of a silky texture, the dog's legs, from its hocks and knees to its toes are free of long hair. On the top of the head, the hair is so profuse as to form a fine, silky "top-knot."

Temperament: The Silky Terrier is extremely affable, keen, alert, quick, and responsive.

Skye Terrier

TERRIER GROUP: USA & UK

Origin: This is one of the oldest of Scottish breeds and is named after its homeland, the Hebridean Isle of Skye, which lies off the northwest coast of Scotland. The Skye Terrier moved from its rugged, humble beginnings to become a favorite among the aristocracy, and Queen Victoria was a particular lover of this little dog which she bred in the royal kennels. A famous depiction of a Skye Terrier is featured in the William Nicholson portrait, *Queen Victoria and Skye Terrier*. Although the majority of Skyes are "prick-eared" there is a "drop-eared" variety where the ears hang flat against the skull.

Size & Substance: Ideal height: dogs 10in; bitches slightly smaller.
This is a solidly built breed, full of strength and quality. Its bone is substantial.

Colors: The Skye Terrier may be black, dark or light gray, fawn, or cream — all with black points. Shading of the same color and a lighter undercoat are permitted so long as the dog's nose and ears are black.

Coat: The Skye's outercoat is long, hard, straight, flat, and free from curl, while the undercoat is short, close, soft, and wooly. The body coat hangs straight down each side, with a parting from the head to the tail. The hair on the dog's head should be shorter, mingling with the side locks that surround the ears like a fringe, and its tail must be well feathered.

Temperament: This intrepid dog is quite fearless but good-tempered, loyal, and canny. It is very much a "one-man dog."

Soft Coated Wheaten Terrier

TERRIER GROUP: USA & UK

Origin: The Soft Coated Wheaten Terrier, a native of Ireland, has an abundant coat, the color of ripening wheat, which is a distinguishing characteristic that sets the dog apart from all other terriers. Many people suppose that it is an ancestor of the Kerry Blue but this has no real authentication.

The Kennel Club in England recognized the breed in 1943, and, in 1946, seven puppies were imported into the USA — as far as anyone knows the first of their kind to arrive there. It was not until 1973 that this dog was accepted into the Terrier Group in the United States where it has now become a very popular breed.

Size & Substance: Height at withers: dogs 18-19.5in; bitches slightly less. Weight: dogs 35-45lb; bitches somewhat less.

Colors: The distinctive coat should be a good clean wheaten — the color of ripening wheat. Dark shading on the ears is also quite typical and permissible.

Coat: This must be soft and silky, neither wooly nor wiry, and loosely waved or with large loose and light curls. An abundant coat covers the dog's body and is especially profuse on the head and legs.

Temperament: The Soft Coated Wheaten Terrier is good tempered, game and spirited. It also displays an affable nature, and is intelligent and full of good humor. Generally, this breed exhibits less aggressiveness than is sometimes encouraged in other terriers.

Spaniels

SPORTING GROUP: USA/GUNDOG GROUP: UK

American Cocker Spaniel
Origin: This New World variety of dog was derived in the last century from the Cocker Spaniel, ostensibly to retrieve quail, and it is a more robust breed than the English version with a prominent rounding of the skull that is distinctive. The English Cocker was itself derived from the oldest of the recognized land spaniels, the Spanish Spaniel, and the name comes from the use of these dogs to hunt woodcock.

When the Cocker Spaniel was brought to the United States in the late 1870s, the American Cocker was developed along different lines from the English Cocker and, in 1946, the two varieties became separate breeds with interbreeding between the two no longer allowed. The American Cocker is the smallest member of the Sporting Group in the USA.

Size & Substance: Ideal height: dogs 14.5-15.5in; bitches 13.5-14.5in.

Colors: Three distinct varieties exist:

Black American Cocker: Includes black with tan points.
Parti-colored American Cocker. Two or more colors with the base color being white.
ASCOB: Any Solid Color Other than Black. This includes those with tan points.

Coat: The coat of the American Cocker Spaniel is its most characteristic attribute. This is silky, and flat, though it may be slightly wavy. Around the head the hair is short and fine, on the body it is of medium length with enough undercoat to give protection, and the ears, chest,

AMERICAN COCKER SPANIEL

abdomen, and legs should be well feathered.

Temperament: Equable and bold, the breed is known as the "merry" Cocker and this description captures the very essence of the breed.

American Water Spaniel

Origin: This breed was probably descended from a mix including Irish Water Spaniels that were brought to the US by immigrants and settlers. These spaniels, along with the Irish Water Spaniels, are the greatest specialists of the family — they excel in water retrieving. However, they were the first breed to be developed in the United States as an all-around hunter that could both retrieve from boats and work ground with relative ease. Initially, little attention was paid to stabilizing the Water Spaniel as a breed until, late in the 19th century, Dr Pheifer, a keen breeder, created a written Standard and applied to the AKC for recognition. The American Water Spaniel was finally admitted to the registry in 1940.

Size & Substance: Height: 15-18in. Weight: dogs 30-45lb; bitches 25-40lb.

This is a solidly built breed; well-muscled with as much substance and bone as necessary to carry the muscular structure but not so much as to appear clumsy.

Colors: The American Water Spaniel may be solid liver, brown, or dark chocolate. A little white on the toes and chest is also permissible.

Coat: This breed's coat can be anything from marcel (uniform waves) to closely curled. Its undercoat provides sufficient density to protect against weather, water, or punishing cover, and is neither too coarse nor too soft. The forehead is covered with short smooth hair and the tail has moderate feathering.

Temperament: The American Water Spaniel is an intelligent dog, with a charming eagerness to please and all-round affability. It also has great energy and an enthusiasm for the hunt, yet is controllable in the field.

Clumber Spaniel

Origin: This versatile hunting dog is believed to have originated in France over 200 years ago and was named for the Clumber Estate of the Duke of Newcastle after the Duc de Noailles moved his kennel to England for sanctuary during the French Revolution. Due to its popularity with the retired military and civil servants, it soon became known as "the retired gentleman's shooting dog." The Clumber became even more fashionable after Britain's King Edward VII and, later, his son George V, kept them at their Sandringham Kennels.

It was first shown in England in 1859 and first registered with the American Kennel Club in 1878, 44 years after the first Clumbers arrived on the North American continent in Nova Scotia.

Size & Substance: USA height at withers: dogs 19-20in; bitches 17-19in. Weight: dogs 70-85lb; bitches 55-70lb. UK weight: dogs 55-70lb; bitches 45-60lb.

Colors: It is preferred that, if marked, the Clumber's plain white body shows lemon markings, though orange is also permissable and the dog might also possess slight head markings and a freckled muzzle. On the body, the general rule is the fewer markings the better, although a spot near the root of the tail is common.

Coat: The Clumber's coat is abundant, close, silky, and straight with a good weather-resistant texture. The chest and legs are well feathered, as are the ears to a lesser extent.

Temperament: This is a steady, reliable, and dignified breed, which is usually friendly but can be more aloof than other spaniels.

English Cocker Spaniel / Cocker Spaniel
Origin: This is undoubtedly the best known and loved of the Spaniels and although originally a hunter is today more of a luxury dog. Literary references to spaniels go back to the days of Chaucer in the 12th century and to Shakespeare, but it was not until the middle of the 19th century that more definition was brought to the spaniel family through selective breeding. Initially, they were differentiated by weight — dogs over 25lb were referred to as Field Spaniels, and those under this weight were designated as Cocker Spaniels. The "cocking spaniel," or Cocker, derived its name from its practice of flushing woodcocks.

The English Cocker Spaniel Club of America was formed, in 1935, to promote the interests of the English Cocker, which had already been recognized as a variety of Cocker Spaniel but not a separate breed and, in 1946, it duly became recognized as a separate breed by the AKC and is now one America's favorite pure-bred dogs.

Size & Substance: USA maximum height: dogs 17in; bitches 16in. UK maximum height: dogs 16in; bitches 15in. Approximate weight: 28-32lb. This breed should be solidly built with as much bone and substance as possible without becoming cloddy or coarse.

COCKER SPANIEL

Colors: Various colors and patterns occur in the Cocker and these are closely regulated. In self colors, for example, no white should appear except on chest. Parti-colors are either clearly marked, ticked, or roaned, and the white appears in combination with black, liver, or shades of red. Solid colors consist of black, liver, or shades of red, and tan markings, clearly defined and of a rich shade, may appear in conjunction with black, liver, and parti-color combinations of those colors. Black and tans and liver and tans are both considered to be solid colors.

Coat: The Cocker's coat is flat and silky — it should never be wiry, curly, wavy, or too profuse. Substantial feathering should appear on the forelegs, body, and hindlegs above the hocks, while on the head, the dog's hair is short and fine.

Temperament: The English Cocker Spaniel is a gentle and affectionate companion though a little spirited and prone to mischief on occasion.

English Springer Spaniel

Origin: The name, Springer, is derived from the way birds spring upwards into the air when startled by this spaniel. This dog had been evolving for a long time from the larger sporting spaniels and was known for a while as the Norfolk Spaniel, after one of the Dukes of Norfolk in the 19th century who was developing the strain. In 1902, the English Springer was given a separate place from its Welsh counterpart in the British Kennel Club Stud Book. Today, the breed in America has diverged so much from the English version that there are strong arguments being put forward for them to be classified as separate breeds in the same way as the Cocker Spaniel.

Size & Substance: Approximate height at shoulder: dogs 20in; bitches 19in. Approximate weight: dogs 50lb; bitches 40lb.
The Springer is a well-knit and sturdy dog, with good bone.

Colors: In the UK, liver and white and black and white are accepted and either of these colors may have additional tan markings. The USA, on the other hand, allows black or liver with white markings or predominantly white with black or liver markings as well as blue or liver roan. Tricolor is also acceptable and should be black and white or liver and white with tan markings. Any white portion of the coat may be flecked with ticking.

Coat: The Springer's outercoat is weather-resistant, of medium length, and may be flat or wavy. The undercoat, is short, soft, and dense. Moderate feathering appears on the ears, forelegs, body, and hindquarters.

Temperament: Friendly and compliant with a happy disposition, this is the ideal working dog for the rough shooter as it will work tirelessly all day and is willing to enter the water even if it has to break the ice to do so.

Field Spaniel
Origin: A product of crossing the Sussex Springer and the Cocker Spaniel in the late 19th century, the Field Spaniel is one of the oldest of land spaniels and the epitome of the basic spaniel. From the early 1880s, when Cocker Spaniels were introduced into America, until 1901, the sole distinction between the Field and Cocker Spaniels was one of size — all dogs under 25lb were classified as Cockers with the bigger dogs being classified as Field Spaniels. However, the breed went into dramatic decline during the 1930s and during World War II, and was almost lost by the end of the 1950s. Today, all modern Field Spaniels are descended from just four dogs.

Size & Substance: Approximate height at shoulders: dogs18in; bitches 17in. Weight: 40-55lb.
This is another solidly built breed, with moderate bone and firm smooth muscles.

Colors: Black, liver, or roan or any of these with tan markings. White is allowed on the throat, chest, and/or brisket, and may be clear, ticked, or roaned on a self color dog.

Coat: The Field Spaniel has a dense and weather-resistant coat. This should be long, flat, glossy, and silky in texture and never curly, short, or wiry. There is abundant feathering on the dog's chest, under the body, and behind the legs.

Temperament: Independent, active, sensitive, and extremely docile.

Irish Water Spaniel
Origin: The Irish Water Spaniel is a breed of great antiquity and was known in the 12th century as the "Shannon Spaniel," "Rat-Tail Spaniel," or "Whip-Tail Spaniel." The smooth "rat" tail, thick at the root and covered for two or three inches with short curls before tapering to a fine point, is a striking characteristic of the breed. It is the tallest of all the spaniels and is often called the clown of the family, possibly due to the distinctive peak of curly hair between the eyes.

Size & Substance: Height: dogs 21-23in; bitches 20-22in. Weight: dogs 55-65lb, bitches 45-58lb.
As with other spaniel breeds, this dog is strongly built and well boned.

Color: The Irish Water Spaniel is unique in that its coat is colored a rich dark liver with a purplish tint or bloom that is peculiar to the breed. This is sometimes referred to as puce-liver.

Coat: The breed's double coat has dense, tight, crisp ringlets, free from wooliness, with an oily texture. On the skull there is a covering of long curls forming a pronounced "top-knot" growing to a well defined peak between the ears.

Temperament: The Irish Water Spaniel is a staunch and affectionate friend although initially aloof. It possesses an endearing sense of humor and is an enthusiastic and intelligent retriever who loves the water — traits that it has inherited from the Poodle which undoubtedly played a large part in its development.

Sussex Spaniel

Origin: The Sussex Spaniel is named after the county in England where the first and most important kennel of these dogs was established as far back as the middle of the 18th century.

The Sussex Spaniel was among the first ten breeds to be recognized and admitted to the Stud Book when the American Kennel Club was formed in 1884. It is somewhat unusual among gundogs in that it tends to give tongue ("speaking") when working and the rich golden liver color is unique to the breed. The Sussex Spaniel continues today essentially unchanged from its 19th century forebears and really deserves more general acclaim than has been its lot of recent years.

Size & Substance: UK Ideal height at withers: 15-16in. Approximate weight: 50lb. USA height at withers: 13-15in. Weight: 35-45lb.
This is a muscular, massive breed.

Colors: The Sussex Spaniel is distinguished by the rich golden liver color that is unique to the breed. This shades to golden at the tip of the hair.

Coat: The breed has an abundant coat, which is flat with no tendency to curl, and an ample undercoat for weather resistance. Its ears are covered with soft, wavy hair and the tail is thickly clothed but not feathered.

FIELD SPANIEL

Temperament: The Sussex Spaniel is extremely affable despite its somber and serious expression.

Welsh Springer Spaniel

Origin: There are obvious similarities between the two breeds of Springer Spaniels but it would be totally untrue to suggest that the Welsh in any way originated from the English variety. It has been suggested that the origins of the Welsh Springer Spaniel can be traced as far back as the arrival of the Gauls to Wales in pre-Roman times and credence can be given to this theory by certain similarities to the Brittany.

Size & Substance: Approximate height at withers: dogs 19in; bitches 18in. The dog's weight should be in proportion to its height and overall balance.

Colors: Rich red and white only.

Coat: The Welsh Springer Spaniel's coat is straight or flat with a silky texture that is never wiry or wavy, but must be sufficiently dense to be waterproof, thornproof, and weatherproof. The back of the forelegs, the hind legs above the hocks, the chest and underside of the body are moderately feathered and light feathering also appears on the ears and tail.

Temperament: With a kindly disposition, the Welsh Springer Spaniel makes a loyal and affectionate companion although it may be reserved with strangers.

Staffordshire Bull Terrier

TERRIER GROUP: USA & UK

Origin: It is generally accepted that the breed evolved in the British Isles from a cross between a Bulldog and a smooth-coated terrier, and was developed for the cruel "sport" of dog-fighting when bull and bear baiting was banned in 1835. Although public opinion turned against this practice, the dog fights continued in Staffordshire, a haven for fighting breeds, for many years and, during the 1850s, American afficionados of dog fighting imported great numbers of dogs from the Midlands of England.

Size & Substance: Desirable height at withers: 14-16in. Weight: dogs 28-38lb; bitches 24-34lb. The weight of these dogs is closely related to their height.

Colors: Red, fawn, white, black, blue, and brindle are all accepable and any of these colors may be marked with white.

Coat: This is invariably smooth, short, and close.

Temperament: The Staffordshire Bull Terrier is a bold, fearless, loyal, and totally reliable dog. Despite its historical reputation for fighting, it is kindness personified with humans and is today one of the most popular of all the terriers.

Tibetan Spaniel

NON-SPORTING GROUP: USA/UTILITY GROUP: UK

Origin: The origins of this dog lie in the isolated Tibetan villages and monastries high in the Himalayan Mountains where they were initially bred by Buddhist monks. The breed first appeared in England in the 1890s and, like the other Tibetan breeds, has greatly increased in popularity since the end of World War II. The Tibetan Spaniel was recognized by the AKC in 1984.

Size & Substance: Approximate height: 10in. Ideal weight: 9-15lb.

Colors: All colors and mixtures of colors are permissable.

Coat: The Tibetan Spaniel has a double coat with the top coat being flat, of moderate length, and silky in texture, while the undercoat is fine and dense. Smooth on the face and front of its legs, its ears and the back of the forelegs are nicely feathered. The tail and buttocks are well furnished with longer hair.

Temperament: This breed is alert, highly intelligent, and loyal. However it is quite independent and may be aloof with strangers.

Tibetan Terrier

NON-SPORTING GROUP: USA/UTILITY GROUP: UK

Origin: This breed evolved over many centuries, in remote sections of the high Himalayas, surviving in extreme climates and difficult terrain, and was thought to bring good luck to anyone who owned one. Travelers to these inacessable places were often given a dog to safeguard them on their journey but these dogs were never sold, as the owners did not want to tempt fate by selling their "luck." The Tibetan people never selectively bred dogs so this terrier has evolved naturally, purely for survival, adapting to one of the harshest environments in the world.

In the UK, the Tibetan Terrier and the Lhasa Apso were originally classified as one breed — the Lhasa Terrier.

Size & Substance: Height at shoulders: dogs 15-16in; bitches slightly smaller. Average weight: 20-24lb.
The proportion of weight to height is far more important than specific weight.

Colors: The recognized colors of this breed are white, golden, cream, gray or smoke, and black. Parti-colors and tricolors are also permitted and can consist of any color except chocolate or liver.

Coat: Due to the extreme climate that the Tibetan Terrier must endure, it possesses a double coat. The top coat is profuse and fine, but not silky nor wooly. It is long, and either straight or waved but not curled and the undercoat is fine and wooly.

Temperament: This is a spirited, alert, and intelligent dog, which is devoted and loyal, though it may be cautious or reserved with strangers.

Vizslas/Hungarian Vizslas

SPORTING GROUP: USA/GUNDOG GROUP: UK

Origin: The Vizsla (also called a Hungarian Pointer) is very popular in its native land. It is possible that the breed can be traced back to the Magyar invasion of Hungary in the tenth century as etchings from that time depict a breed very similar to today's Vizslas.

Through the centuries this sporting gundog has been used with great success in the hunting of game birds and hare on the ranging plains of its homeland and Hungarians who fled their homeland between the two World Wars took their beloved pointers with them. Now a respected breed, the Vizsla, which is known in the UK as the Hungarian Vizsla, was registered in the USA in 1960.

Size & Substance: Height at withers: dogs 22-24in; bitches 21-23in. Weight: 48lb 7oz-66lb.

Colors: Russet gold is the most common color for this bred but it can be shaded from rusty gold to dark sandy yellow. The nose, lips, and eye rims are brown and eye color should harmonize with the coat color.

Coat: The Vizsla's coat will feel greasy to the touch and should be short, straight, dense, smooth, and shiny.

Temperament: This is a lively, gentle-mannered, yet fearless breed that will be affectionate with a well-developed protective instinct.

Weimaraner

SPORTING GROUP: USA/GUNDOG GROUP: UK

Origin: This striking, noble dog is another of the multi-purpose hunt, point, and retrieve dogs originating in continental Europe and dates back to the early 19th century in Weimar, Germany. The breed was developed to stalk deer, bear, and wild boar from the old red Schweisshunde that was responsible for a great number of Germany's hunting dogs. It is likely that it was perfected from crosses between the German Shorthaired Pointer and native hunting breeds.

This all-round hunting companion, fondly known as the "Gray Ghost" in America, was recognized by the AKC in 1943 and has become very popular with the shooting fraternity in Britain over the last 20 years.

Size & Substance: USA height at withers: dogs 25-27in; bitches 23-25in. UK height at withers: dogs 24-27in; bitches 22-25in. Weight: dogs up to 85lb; bitches up to 70lb.

Colors: The Weimaraner should preferably be silver-gray in color, but shades of mouse or roe gray are also permissible. The whole coat gives a metallic sheen and shades blend to a lighter color on the head and ears. There is frequently a dark eel stripe along the back, and a small white mark on the chest is also allowed.

Coat: Two coat lengths are seen in this breed; the smooth is short, smooth, and sleek, while the longhaired variety has long hair on the body, somewhat longer on neck, chest, and belly with feathering on the tail and the back of the legs. The longhaired is, however, not recognized by the AKC.

Temperament: The Weimaraner is fearless and affable, protective, alert, and compliant.

Welsh Corgis

HERDING GROUP: USA/WORKING GROUP: UK

Cardigan Welsh Corgi

Origin: Corgis are very agile and sturdy dogs that are reputed to have been used in Wales for pony and sheep herding in the distant past. The Corgi type dog was brought to Wales by the Celts about 1200 BC and called the "Yard Long Dog" (Ci Llathaid).

Popular belief is that the breed is descended from early Dachshunds. Both the Cardigan and the Pembroke derive from common stock and were not distinguished officially as separate breeds until the mid 1930s. In stark contrast to the Pembroke, the Cardigan may be almost any color, bearing testimony to its more varied ancestry.

Size & Substance: Ideal height at shoulder: 12in. Ideal weight: dogs 30-38lb; bitches 25-34lb.

Weight should be in proportion to the dog's size with overall balance the prime consideration.

Colors: The Cardigan may be any color, with or without white markings, although the white should not predominate. White flashings are usual on the neck, chest, legs, muzzle, underparts, tip of tail, and as a blaze on the head.

Coat: The double, weather-resistant coat of the Cardigan Welsh Corgi consists of a top coat that is medium length, strong, and hard textured — never wiry, curly, or silky. The insulating undercoat is short, soft, and there is thick, short hair on the ears, head, and the legs as well as slightly longer, thicker hair in the dog's ruff, on the backs of the thighs to form "pants," and on the underside of the tail.

CARDIGAN CORGI

Temperament: The Cardigan Welsh Corgi is an alert, steady, intelligent, loyal, and affectionate breed.

Pembroke Welsh Corgi

Origin: The Pembroke, brought to Wales in AD 1107 by Flemish weavers, was originally bred to herd cattle by nipping at their heels. The breed is thought to have originated from a Spitz variety, unlike the Cardigan (Dachshund), and it had to be agile and nimble enough to avoid the kicking hooves of the animals it was herding. The Pembroke Welsh Corgi is the smallest dog in the herding group and the name corgi means "dwarf dog" in the Welsh language. It has been suggested that all working dogs in Wales were once called "corgi" and this is borne out by the appellation of the Pembroke and the Cardigan — both Welsh dogs, originally of no relation, but both called corgis.

Since they were distinguished as two separate breeds in the 1930s they have remained pure and their respective breed types have become more clearly defined. The Pembroke's high level of popularity today is undoubtedly because of its favor with the current British Royal Family, and particularly with Queen Elizabeth II who adores the breed above all others.

Size & Substance: Height at shoulder: 10-12ins. Weight: dogs 22-26lb; bitches 20-24lb.
Weight is in proportion to size and the Pembroke Welsh Corgi should not be so low and heavy-boned as to appear coarse or overdone, nor so light-boned as to appear racy.

Colors: This breed is made up of the self colors — red, sable, fawn, and black and tan — with or without white markings on neck, brisket, and legs.

Coat: This is strong, medium-long, straight, and flat with a dense, weather-resistant undercoat that should never be soft, wavy, or wiry. The hair is slightly longer on the back of the dog's forelegs and its underparts, and somewhat fuller and longer on the rear of the dog's hindquarters.

Temperament: Spirited and affable.

Welsh Terrier

TERRIER GROUP: USA & UK

Origin: This dog may well have common ancestry with the Lakeland Terrier as prior to the Roman invasion of Britain its Celtic owners took to the hills of the Lake District and the mountains of Wales. Originally known as the Old English Terrier or Black and Tan Wire Haired Terrier, this extremely courageous, all-round gundog would not hesitate to stand up to a large wild beast.

Size & Substance: Maximum height at shoulder: dogs 15.5in; bitches may be proportionally smaller. Weight: 20-21lb.
This is a solid dog, of good substance.

Colors: The Welsh Terrier should preferably be black and tan, or black grizzle and tan, free from black pencilling on the toes. The jacket is black, spreading up onto the neck, down onto the tail, and into the upper thighs. The legs, quarters, and head are clear tan. The tan is a deep reddish color, with slightly lighter shades being acceptable. A grizzle jacket is also acceptable but not preferred.

Coat: Abundant, wiry, hard and very close with a short, soft undercoat. Furnishings on the muzzle, legs, and quarters are dense and wiry.

Temperament: This breed is an affable and boisterous companion, which shows marked intelligence and compliance. Game and fearless, it is able to hold its own when the situation demands.

West Highland White Terrier

TERRIER GROUP: USA & UK

Origin: Originally registered as the Roseneath Terrier, the first AKC registration was in 1908, and the name was officially changed to West Highland White Terrier in 1909.

This most Scottish of dogs is one of the most popular of the terrier breeds. According to canine historians, the breed originated at Poltalloch, Scotland with the Malcolm family, and it is probable that the lineage of the Malcolm dogs goes back to the time of King James I, who asked for some "earth-dogges" out of Argyleshire. The story goes that in the early 1900s, Colonel Malcolm accidently shot one of his favorite dogs, a reddish-brown terrier, mistaking it for a fox, and so decreed from then on that only white terriers would be bred in his kennel. It is highly likely that the West Highland White Terrier came from the same stock as the Scotties, Cairns, and the Dandie Dinmonts.

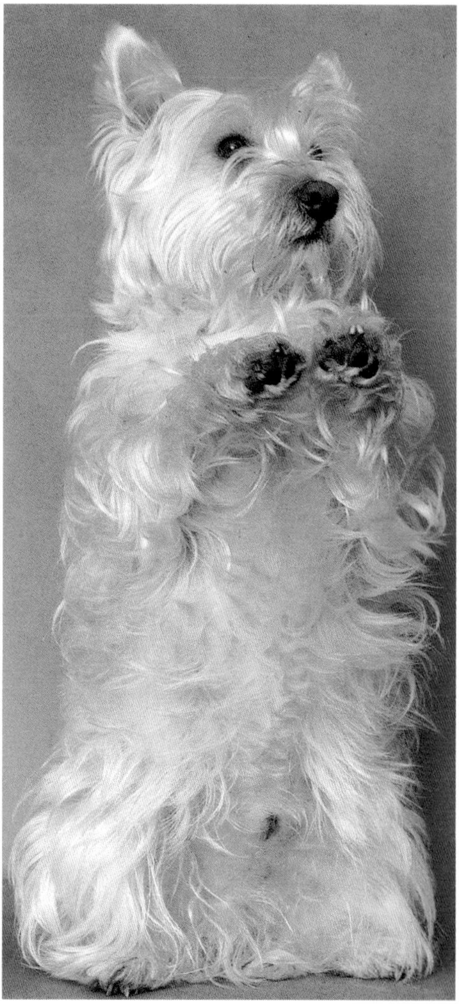

Size & Substance: Approximate height at withers: dogs 11in; bitches 10in.
A good example of a West Highland White Terrier will be compact and fine boned.

Colors: White only.

Coat: The West Highland White Terrier's double coat consists of a harsh outercoat that is long and free from curl and an undercoat that resembles fur — short, soft, and close. Furnishings may be somewhat softer and longer but should never give the appearance of fluff. Considerable hair is left around the head to act as a frame for the face, giving a typical Westie expression.

Temperament: Alert, sprightly, courageous, self-reliant, and affable.

Whippet

HOUND GROUP: USA & UK

Origin: The Whippet was originally bred as a sighthound to pursue and capture small game. It looks much like a miniature Greyhound in appearance, and, like its bigger cousin, is a powerful racing dog. Whereas there is little argument that the Greyhound has existed as a breed for thousands of years, opinions vary wildly as to the origins of the Whippet. Some historians argue that early paintings and pottery depict the breed dating back to the fifth century AD while others aver that the Whippet only came into being in the late 19th century when small Greyhounds were bred with terriers to produce a fast little hunting dog.

Whippets are thought to have been brought to the USA by the English mill operatives of Massachusetts and, today, the American Standard varies from that of the UK mainly in aspects of height, front, and shoulder construction, eye color, and pigmentation.

Size & Substance: USA ideal height at withers: dogs 19-22in; bitches 18-21in. UK height at withers: dogs 18.5-20in; bitches 17-18.5in.
The Whippet should be lithe, with moderate bone throughout its frame.

Colors: Any color or mixture of colors is acceptable.

Coat: This should be fine, short, and close in texture.

Temperament: The Whippet is gentle, affectionate, and steady, but capable of great intensity during sporting pursuits.

Yorkshire Terrier

TOY GROUP: USA & UK

Origin: This manmade creation, although a terrier by nature, is shown in all its glory when presented as a show dog with its perfectly coiffured lustrous coat. The Yorkshire Terrier made its first appearance at a bench show in England in 1861 as a "broken-haired Scotch Terrier." Later, in the 1860s, a woman named Mary Ann Foster began to popularize the breed around the British Isles and one of her dogs named "Huddersfield Ben" is still referred to as the "father of the breed."

The earliest record of a Yorkshire Terrier born in the United States dates to 1872. During the late Victorian era, the Yorkshire Terrier quickly became a popular pet and as Americans embraced Victorian customs they took the Yorkshire Terrier to their hearts where it became an AKC-recognized breed in 1885.

Size & Substance: Maximum weight: 7lb.

Colors: A dark steel blue (not silver blue), extends from the top of the head to the root of the dog's tail and should never be mingled with fawn, bronze, or dark hairs. The chest is a rich bright tan that must be darker at the roots, shading through the middle to lighter at the tips. Around the head is rich golden tan hair, deeper in color at the sides of head, ear roots, and on the muzzle, with the ears themselves being a deep tan. The tan color should not extend down onto the back of the neck. The forelegs are the same bright tan color as the chest but this should not extend above the elbow, or above the stifle on the hind legs.

Coat: The Yorkie's hair is moderately long on the body, glossy, and perfectly straight (never wavy). It should be of a fine silky texture that is not wooly. On the head it is very long and can be tied with one bow in the center of head or parted in the middle and tied with two.

Temperament: The Yorkshire Terrier is a very spirited yet steady character and has lots of personality for its diminutive size.